Karma

The word "karma" in its various interpretations has inevitably become a part of the world's many languages because it names a law which is universal in its operation. To the literal-minded, it may seem nothing more than the inexorable law of cause and effect, binding us forever to the wheel of pain and misery, since every effect simply becomes the cause of another effect. But those who see beneath the surface manifestations of this law can perceive an inner harmony which is never distorted or mutilated by the dissonances of everyday experience. The pendulum swings; the scales tip heavily one way or the other; but there is inevitably a center of balance to which all must return. To find that center as an inner reality is the goal of every thinking person. In this sense, then, karma is seen as the rhythmic balancing of life's forces in such a manner that cause-effect are one, and at every moment the action is right, complete, harmonious.

This book examines the law of karma from various points of view, each enriched and made meaningful by the writer's own authentic experience. Several of the contributions appeared originally in a special issue of *The American Theosophist* dealing with "Reincarnation and Karma," but the emphasis here is on the universal principle of Karma which maintains the balance of nature and of our individual lives.

KARMA

The Universal Law of Harmony

Edited
by
VIRGINIA HANSON

A QUEST BOOK

Published under a grant from the Kern Foundation

THE THEOSOPHICAL PUBLISHING HOUSE
Wheaton, Ill., U.S.A.
Madras, India / London, England

Original Quest Book edition published by the
Theosophical Publishing House, Wheaton, Illinois, a
department of The Theosophical Society in America

Library of Congress Cataloging in Publication Data

Hanson, Virginia.
  Karma.

    (A Quest book)
    1. Karma.   I. Title.
BP573.K3H3   291.2   74-18957
ISBN 0-8356-0462-4

PRINTED IN THE UNITED STATES OF AMERICA

CONTENTS

FOREWORD

Action is as natural to man as breathing. To breathe, ultimately, is to act, for the very pulsation of the breath displaces atoms in space, releases energies, and disturbs or reestablishes equilibrium. Breathing but mirrors the universal ebb and flow of all cyclic processes, and in the act of breathing we reaffirm our connection with the universal. The rhythm of inbreathing and out-breathing—inhalation and exhalation—should give us a clue to all action: whatever goes out must eventually turn upon itself for a return journey inwards; whatever moves within must one day be given *ex*pression.

Man has always pondered the nature of his action, seeking either to escape the consequences of his acts or to modify the results in such a manner as to insure no harm will come to him. To accept full responsibility for all our choices, and hence for all our actions, requires often more courage than we possess and maturity we long to achieve yet seemingly cannot attain. Only when the outcome of our choices is happy do we claim credit for right action; when the consequence is painful, we are quick to deny any association with the causative factors, attributing the outcome to circumstances or our genetic structure.

Choice—self-conscious choice—is a specifically human capability; to abrogate our right to choose be-tween alternatives, even the right to say no to all choices, is to forfeit some part of our humanity. To permit others to make our choices for us is in itself a choice, and we must still pay the price demanded by the conse-quences of our default. Every moment of every day presents us with innumerable choices: what we shall think, what we shall feel, what we shall do. At times it may appear we are chosen by our thoughts or emotions, but this is only because we have permitted the mind or the heart to move without conscious direction, a choice

which can be reversed whenever we decide to determine consciously what thoughts will occupy the mind or
what feelings will be harbored in the heart.

  Out of our choices, then, arises the complex pattern
of our existence, each choice weaving the invisible web
of circumstances in which we find ourselves enmeshed.
Inherent in every action is the burden of its consequence, for action and reaction are ever polarized in
life itself. All the great religious traditions have recognized this basic polarity. For the Buddhist, the re-
current cycles of birth and death are subject to the law
of interdependent origination, recognizing that the
wheel is turned by man's own hand; for the Hindu, the
inexorable law of *karma*, action which ever turns upon
itself in reaction, operates throughout the universe; for
the Christian, the assurance that "whatsoever ye sow
that shall ye also reap" is affirmation of a lawfulness
pervading all universal processes. Throughout all nature, the interconnectedness of life in its manifold
forms is evidenced, a universal law of harmony revealing itself again and again in innumerable patterns. If
our own lives seem exempt from the harmonic law, it is
but a lack of adequate perspective from which to view
events. We may be too close in time or too near in space
to observe with any accuracy or understanding the outcome of our choices, but to say law is not operative or
pattern is not to be found is to fail to perceive the larger
truth that order could not be anywhere were it not
everywhere, harmony could not be achieved were
lawfulness a sometime thing.

  Action, of course, is more than physical movement; it
is emotion and thought as well. The lawfulness of consequence, therefore, is as much a moral principle as it is
applicable to the physical realm of existence. The complexity of the web we weave is thereby enhanced, for
motive, strength of thought or feeling, intentionality,
all play their part in creating the outcome of any event
or act. Karma, as the universal law that equilibrizes and

harmonizes action and reaction, is not a "tit-for-tat" game; it is the universal dynamic constantly operative at every level, interweaving motive and act, intent and desire, motion and emotion. Ever adjusting, the law is both purposeful and merciful, for it is not the law which rewards or punishes, but we who by our choices bear both the joys and sorrows of those choices, weaving the patterns of our cyclic progress from nescience to omniscience as we mount the ladder of consciousness in the unfoldment of our divine potential.

One of the major contributions of The Theosophical Society has been the reintroduction into the western world of the long neglected and often forgotten concept of cyclic progression in accordance with universal law. The Sanskrit term, *karma*, has been adopted in English dictionaries as the all-embracing term for that universal law, the harmonic law of adjustment or compensation, action-reaction, to which all natural processes are subject. The ramifications of the law must be as endless and complex as those processes; yet in its ultimate simplicity, the law is harmony, the perfect relationship which obtains between all things everywhere. And as relationship, the law, finally, is known as love, the one true and abiding relationship in the universe.

In the essays that follow, comprising in this brief volume a survey of the meaning and nature of karma, various aspects of the universal law, the harmonics of love in action throughout the universe, are touched upon. But, as the Pseudo-Dionysius put it: "Man must not only learn the truth; he must suffer it." So our very lives give evidence of the patterns of the law, if we could but see, and when we learn to weave all patterns with the light of love, the fabric of existence will be luminous and our every act reflect the harmony of the divine.

—JOY MILLS

1.

Karma—The Womb of Time

A selection of quotations from the works
of H .P. Blavatsky.
LINA PSALTIS, Compiler

Karma as generally understood in the Western world
is a rather vague term coming from the Eastern religious meaning, usually, a simplistic, when not moronic,
idea that one has "good things or bad things" happening to him. H. P. Blavatsky, when writing upon this
subject in the late 19th century had this to say when
asked how theosophical principles can be applied to
everyday living:

> Let me briefly remind you what these principles
> are—universal Unity and Causation; Human Soli-
> darity; the Law of Karma; re-incarnation. These are
> the four links of the golden chain which should bind
> humanity into one family, one universal
> Brotherhood.[1]

The following quotations selected from her works are
an effort to help the student find his way through the
maze of life as it exists within the womb of time. It is only
within the boundaries of our own individual experiences in life that we can arrive at a satisfying sense of
where in space and time we exist.

****

[The following definition as given in the *Theosophical
Glossary* involves terms unfamiliar, perhaps, to many
readers. However, in order to cover as much ground as
possible they have been left undefined. It is to be hoped

that the interested student will find them intriguing enough that more study will follow.]*

Karma (Sk.). Physically, action: metaphysically, the Law of Retribution, the Law of cause and effect or Ethical Causation. Nemesis, only in one sense, that of bad Karma. It is the eleventh *Nidana* in the concatenation of causes and effects in orthodox Buddhism; yet it is the power that controls all things, the resultant of moral action, the metaphysical *Samskâra*, or the moral effect of an act committed for the attainment of something which gratifies a personal desire. There is the Karma of merit and the Karma of demerit. Karma neither punishes nor rewards, it is simply *the one* Universal Law which guides unerringly, and, so to say, blindly, all other laws productive of certain effects along the grooves of their respective causations. When Buddhism teaches* that "Karma is that moral kernel (of any being) which alone survives death and continues in transmigration" or reincarnation, it simply means that there remains nought after each Personality but the causes produced by it; causes which are undying, i.e., which cannot be eliminated from the Universe until replaced by their legitimate effects, and wiped out by them, so to speak, and such causes—unless compensated during the life of the person who produced them with adequate effects, will follow the reincarnated Ego, and reach it in its subsequent reincarnation until a hammony between effects and causes is fully reestablished. No "personality"—a mere bundle of material atoms and of instinctual and mental characteristics—can of course continue, as such, in the world of pure Spirit. Only that which is immortal in its very nature and divine in its essence, namely, the Ego, can exist for ever. And it is that Ego which chooses the personality it will inform, after each Devachan, and which receives through these per-

*All bracketed words in the following material are those of the compiler.

[*Readers who have not encountered this in their study of Buddhism are referred to the teachings of the Mahayana School.]

sonalities the effects of the Karmic causes produced,
it is therefore the Ego, that *self* which is the "moral
kernel" referred to and embodied karma, "which
alone survives death."[2]

[Karma, conceptually, cannot be separated from the
concept of *Dharma. Dharma* is translated many ways,
such as: duty, righteousness, mercy, etc. From dharma
and karma, we arrive at the earliest known concept, and
that is rta. All of these terms evolved in the richness of
the Indian mind from a period perhaps pre-Vedic,
hence possibly before the third millenium B.C. These
philosophic teachings regarding the moral nature of
man and the universe can then be read knowing that
more than 5000 years of deliberation, contemplation
and experimentation are involved.]

****

... The law of Karma is a moral law, and where no
moral responsibility exists, there can be no application of the law of Karma; but the law of cause and
effect applies to all departments of nature.[3]

****

... Exoteric religions base their morality on the hope
of reward and fear of punishment at the hands of an
Omnipotent Ruler of the Universe by following the
rules he has at his pleasure laid down for the obedience of his helpless subjects; in some cases, however,
religions of later growth have made morality to depend on the sentiment of gratitude to that Ruler for
benefits received.[4]

****

... There is one eternal Law in nature, one that
always tends to adjust contraries and to produce final
harmony. It is owing to this law of spiritual development superseding the physical and purely intellectual, that mankind will become freed from its false
gods, and find itself finally—SELF-REDEEMED.[5]

****

Karma is a word of many meanings, and has a special term for almost every one of its aspects. It means, as a synonym of sin, the performance of some action for the attainment of an object of *worldly,* hence *selfish,* desire, which cannot fail to be hurtful to somebody else. Karma is action, the Cause; and Karma again is "the law of ethical causation"; the *effect* of an act produced egotistically, when the great law of harmony depends on altruism.[6]

****

... it is only this doctrine, we say, that can explain to us the mysterious problem of Good and Evil, and reconcile man to the terrible and *apparent* injustice of life. Nothing but such certainty can quiet our revolted sense of justice. For, when one unacquainted with the noble doctrine looks around him, and observes the inequalities of birth and fortune, of intellect and capacities; when one sees honour paid fools and profligates, on whom fortune has heaped her favours by mere privilege of birth, and their nearest neighbour, with all his intellect and noble virtues —far more deserving in every way—perishing of want and for lack of sympathy; when one sees all this and has to turn away, helpless to relieve the undeserved suffering, one's ears ringing and heart aching. . . that blessed knowledge of Karma alone prevents him from cursing life and men. . . .[7]

[The reality of man's inner powers and energies has become inherent to the culture of Western man. This awareness entails many other elements, such as a terminology within which we can communicate. The following selection serves this purpose]:

... To understand the idea [of reincarnation and karma] well you have to first study the dual sets of "principles": the *spiritual,* or those which belong to the imperishable Ego; and the *material,* or those principles which make up the ever-changing bodies or the series of personalities of that Ego. Let us fix permanent these, and say that:—

I. *Atma*, the *"Higher Self,"* is neither your Spirit nor mine, but like sunlight shines on all. It is the universally diffused *"divine principle,"* and is inseparable from its one and absolute *Meta*-Spirit, as the sunbeam is inseparable from sunlight.

II. *Buddhi* (the spiritual soul) is only its vehicle. Neither each separately, nor the two collectively, are of any more use to the body of man, than sunlight and its beams are for a mass of granite buried in the earth, *unless the divine Duad is assimilated by, and reflected in*, some *consciousness*. Neither Atma nor Buddhi is ever reached by Karma, because the former is the highest aspect of Karma, *its working agent* of Itself in one aspect, and the other is unconscious *on this plane*. *This consciousness or mind is,*

III. *Manas,** the derivation or product in a reflected form of *Ahamkara*, "the conception of I," or Egoship. It is, therefore, when inseparably united to the first two, called the Spiritual Ego, and *Taijasi* (the radiant). This is the real Individuality, or the divine man. It is this Ego which—having originally incarnated in the *senseless* human form animated by, but unconscious (since it had no consciousness) of, the presence in itself of the dual monad—made of that human-like form *a real man*. It is that Ego, that "Causal Body," which overshadows every personality Karma forces it to incarnate into; and this Ego, which is held responsible for all the sins committed through, and in, every new body or personality—the evanescent masks which hide the true Individual through the long series of rebirths.

ENQ. But is this just? Why should this Ego receive punishment as the result of deeds which it has forgotten?

THEO. It has not forgotten them, it knows and remembers its misdeeds as well as you remember what you have done yesterday. Is it because the memory of that

---

*Mahat or the "Universal Mind" is the source of Manas. The latter is Mahat, i.e., mind, in man. Manas is also called *Kshetrajna*, "embodied Spirit."

bundle of physical compounds called "body" does not recollect what its predecessor (the personality *that was*) did, that you imagine that the real Ego has forgotten them? As well say it is unjust that the new boots on the feet of a boy, who is flogged for stealing apples, should be punished for that which they know nothing of.

ENQ. But if it is punished in this life for the misdeeds committed in a previous one, then it is this Ego that ought to be rewarded also, whether here, or when disincarnated.

THEO. And so it is. If we do not admit of any punishment outside of this earth, it is because the only state the Spiritual Self knows of, hereafter, is that of unalloyed bliss.

ENQ. What do you mean?

THEO. Simply this: *crimes and sins committed on a plane of objectivity and in a world of matter, cannot receive punishment in a world of pure subjectivity.* We believe in no hell or paradise as localities; in no objective hell-fires and worms that never die, nor in any Jerusalems with streets paved with sapphires and diamonds. What we believe in is a *postmortem state* or mental condition, such as we are in during a vivid dream. We believe in an immutable law of absolute Love, Justice, and Mercy. And believing in it, we say: "Whatever the sin and dire results of the original Karmic transgression of the now incarnated Egos no man (or the outer material and periodical form of the Spiritual Entity) can be held, with any degree of justice, responsible for the consequences of his birth. He does not ask to be born, nor can he choose the parents that will give him life. In every respect he is a victim to his environment, the child of circumstances over which he has no control; and if each of his transgressions were impartially investigated, there would be found nine out of every ten cases when he was the one sinned against, rather than the sinner. Life is at best a heartless play, a stormy sea to cross, and a heavy burden often too difficult to bear. The greatest philosophers have tried in vain to fathom and find out its *raison d'etre*, and have failed except those who had the key to it, namely, the Eastern sages. Life is, as Shakespeare describes it:—

> ".... but a walking shadow—a poor player,
> That struts and frets his hour upon the stage,
> And then is heard no more. It is a tale
> Told by an idiot, full of sound and fury,
> Signifying nothing. . . ."

Nothing in its separate part, yet of the greatest importance in its collectively or series of lives. At any rate, almost every individual life is, in its full development, a sorrow. And are, we to believe that poor, helpless man, after being tossed about like a piece of rotten timber on the angry billows of life, is, if he proves too weak to resist them, to be punished by a *sempiternity* of damnation, or even a temporary punishment? Never! Whether a great or an average sinner, good or bad, guilty or innocent, once delivered of the burden of physical life, the tired and worn-out *Manu* ("thinking Ego") has won the right to a period of absolute rest and bliss. The same unerringly wise and just rather than merciful Law, which inflicts upon the incarnated Ego the Karmic punishment for every sin committed during the preceding life on Earth, provided for the now disembodied Entity a long lease of mental rest, i.e., the entire oblivion of every sad event, aye, to the smallest painful thought, that took place in its last life as a personality, leaving in the soul-memory but the reminiscence of that which was bliss, or led to happiness. Plotinus, who said that our body was the true river of Lethe, for "souls plunged into it forget all," meant more than he said. For, as our terrestrial body is like Lethe, so is our *celestial body* in Devachan, and much more.

ENQ. Then am I to understand that the murderer, the transgressor of law divine and human in every shape, is allowed to go unpunished?

THEO. Who ever said that? Our philosophy has a doctrine of punishment as stern as that of the most rigid Calvinist, only far more philosophical and consistent with absolute justice. No deed, not even a sinful

thought, will go unpunished; the latter more severely
even than the former, as a thought is far more potential in creating evil results than even a deed.* We
believe in an unerring law of Retribution, called
Karma, which asserts itself in a natural concatenation
of causes and their unavoidable results.

ENQ. And how, or where, does it act?

THEO. Every labourer is worthy of his hire, saith
Wisdom . . . [Thus the] "personality" is no better
than a fresh suit of clothes with its specific characteristics, colour, form and qualities; but the *real* man
who wears it is the same culprit as of old. It is the
individuality who suffers through his "personality."
And it is this, and this alone, that can account for the
terrible, still only *apparent*, injustice in the distribu-
tion of lots in life to man. When your modern
philosophers will have succeeded in showing to us a
good reason, why so many apparently innocent and
good men are born only to suffer during a whole
life-time; why so many are born poor unto starvation
in the slums of great cities, abandoned by fate and
men; why, while these are born in the gutter, others
open their eyes to light in palaces; while a noble birth
and fortune seem often given to the worst of men and
only rarely to the worthy; while there are beggars
whose <u>inner</u> selves are peers to the highest and noblest of men; when this, and much more, is satisfac-
torily explained by either your philosophers or
theologians, then only, but not till then, you will have
the right to reject the theory of reincarnation. The
highest and grandest of poets have dimly perceived
this truth of truths. Shelley believed in it, Shakespeare must have thought of it when writing on the
worthlessness of Birth. Remember his words:

"Why should my birth keep down my mounting
spirit?
Are not all creatures subject unto time?
There's legions now of beggars on the earth,

---

*"Verily, I say unto you, that whosoever looketh at a woman to lust after her,
hath committed adultery with her already in his heart." (Matt. 5:28.)

> That their original did spring from Kings,
> And many monarchs now, whose fathers were
> The riff-raff of their age . . . ."

Alter the word "fathers" into "Egos"—and you will
have the truth.[8]

****

ENQ. But what is Karma?

THEO. As I have said, we consider it as the *Ultimate Law* of
the Universe, the source, origin and fount of all other
laws which exist throughout Nature. Karma is the
unerring law which adjusts effect to cause, on the
physical, mental and spiritual planes of being. As no
cause remains without its due effect from greatest to
least, from a cosmic disturbance down to the movement of your hand, and as like produces like, *Karma*
is that unseen and unknown law *which adjusts wisely,
intelligently and equitably* each effect to its cause, trac-
ing the latter back to its producer. Though itself
unknowable, its action is perceivable.

ENQ. Then it is the "Absolute," the "Unknowable" again,
and is not of much value as an explanation of the
problems of life?

THEO. On the contrary. For, though we do not know what
Karma is *per se*, and in its essence, we *do* know *how* it
works, and we can define and describe its mode of
action with accuracy. We only do *not* know its
ullitmate *Cause,* just as modern philosophy universally admits that the *ultimate* Cause of anything is
"unknowable." . . . the particular conditions of life in
which each person finds himself, are nothing more
than the retributive Karma which the individual generated in a previous life. We must not lose sight of the
fact that every atom is subject to the general law
governing the whole body to which it belongs, and
here we come upon the wider track of the Karmic
law. Do you not perceive that the aggregate of individual Karma becomes that of the nation to which
those individuals belong, and further, that the sum
total of National Karma is that of the World? . . . it is
upon this broad line of Human interdependence that

the law of Karma finds its legitimate and equable issue.

ENQ. Do I, then, understand that the law of Karma is not necessarily an individual law?

THEO. That is just what I mean. It is impossible that Karma could readjust the balance of power in the world's life and progress, unless it had a broad and general line of action. It is held as a truth among Theosophists that the interdependence of Humanity is the cause of what is called Distributive Karma, and it is this law which affords the solution to the great question of collective suffering and its relief. It is an occult law, moreover, that no man can rise superior to his individual failings, without lifting, be it ever so little, the whole body of which he is an integral part. In the same way, no one can sin, nor suffer the effects of sin, alone. In reality, there is no such thing as "Separateness"; and the nearest approach to that selfish state, which the laws of life permit, is in the intent or motive. . . . When every individual has contributed to the general good what he can of money, of labour, and of ennobling thought, then, and only then, will the balance of National Karma be struck, and until then we have no right nor any reasons for saying that there is more life on the earth than Nature can support. It is reserved for the heroic souls, the Saviours of our Race and Nation, to find out the cause of this unequal pressure of retributive Karma, and by a supreme effort to re-adjust the balance of power, and save the people from a moral ingulfment a thousand times more disastrous and more permanently evil than the like physical catastrophe, in which you seem to see the only possible outlet for this accumulated misery.

ENQ. Well, then, tell me generally how you describe this law of Karma?

THEO. We describe Karma as that Law of re-adjustment which ever tends to restore disturbed equilibrium in the physical, and broken harmony in the moral world. We say that Karma does not act in this or that particular way always; but that it always *does* act so as to restore Harmony and preserve the balance of equilibrium, in virtue of which the Universe exists.

ENQ. Give me an illustration.

THEO. Later on I will give you a full illustration. Think now of a pond. A stone falls into the water and creates disturbing waves. These waves oscillate backwards and forwards till at last, owing to the operation of what physicists call the law of the dissipation of energy, they are brought to rest, and the water returns to its condition of calm tranquillity. Similarly *all* action, on every plane, produces disturbance in the balanced harmony of the Universe, and the vibrations so produced will continue to roll backwards and forwards, if its area is limited, till equilibrium is restored. But since each such disturbance starts from some particular point, it is clear that equilibrium and harmony can only be restored by the reconverging *to that same point* of all the forces which were set in motion from it. And here you have proof that the consequences of a man's deeds, though, etc. must all react upon *himself* with the same force with which they were set in motion.

ENQ. But I see nothing of a moral character about this law. It looks to me like the simple physical law that action and re-action are equal and opposite.

THEO. I am not surprised to hear you say that. Europeans have got so much into the ingrained habit of considering right and wrong, good and evil, as matters of an arbitrary code of law laid down either by men, or imposed upon them by a Personal God. We Theosophists, however, say that "Good" and "Harmony," and "Evil" and "Dis-harmony," are synonymous. Further we maintain that all pain and suffering are results of want of Harmony, and that the one terrible and only cause of the disturbance of Harmony is *selfishness* in some form or another. Hence Karma gives back to every man the *actual consequences* of his own actions, without any regard to their moral character; but since he receives his due for *all,* it is obvious that he will be made to atone for all sufferings which he has caused, just as he will reap in joy and gladness the fruits of all the happiness and harmony he had helped to produce.[9]

****

THEO. . . . A plant consists of a root, a stem, and many shoots and leaves. As humanity, as a whole, is the stem which grows from the spiritual root, so is the stem the unity of the plant. Hurt the stem and it is obvious that every shoot and leaf will suffer. So it is with mankind.

ENQ. Yes, but if you injure a leaf or a shoot, you do not injure the whole plant.

THEO. And therefore you think that by injuring *one* man you do not injure humanity? But how do *you* know? Are you aware that even materialistic science teaches that any injury, however slight, to a plant will affect the whole course of its future growth and development? Therefore, you are mistaken, and the analogy is perfect. If, however, you overlook the fact that a cut in the finger may often make the whole body suffer, and react on the whole nervous system, I must all the more remind you that there may well be other spiritual laws, operating on plants and animals as well as mankind, although, as you do not recognize their action on plants and animals, you may deny their existence.

ENQ. What laws do you mean?

THEO. We call them Karmic laws; but you will not understand the full meaning of the term unless you study Occultism. However, my argument did not rest on the assumption of these laws, but really on the analogy of the plant. Expand the idea, carry it out to a universal application, and you will soon find that in true philosophy every physical action has its moral and everlasting effect. Hurt a man by doing him bodily harm; you may think that his pain and suffering cannot spread by any means to his neighbours, least of all to men of other nations. We affirm *that it will, in good time.* Therefore, we say, that unless every man is brought to understand and accept *as an axiomatic truth* that by wronging one man we wrong not only ourselves but the whole humanity in the long run, no brotherly feelings such as preached by all the great Reformers, pre-eminently by Buddha and Jesus, are possible on earth.[10]

****

[The following is just a brief statement regarding the science of astrology as it applies to karma]:

... We hold that the science of Astrology only determines the *nature of effects*, by a knowledge of the law of magnetic affinities and attractions of the Planetary bodies, but that it is the *Karma* of the individual himself, which places him in that particular magnetic relation.[11]

****

[The subject of life after death is obviously inextricably bound up with the doctrine of karma. Space allows only these few words]:

THEO. The whole punishment after death, even for the materialist, consists, therefore, in the absence of any reward, and the utter loss of the consciousness of one's bliss and rest. Karma is the child of the terrestrial Ego, the fruit of the actions of the tree which is the objective personality visible to all, as much as the fruit of all the thoughts and even motives of the spiritual "I"; but Karma is also the tender mother, who heals the wounds inflicted by her during the preceding life, before she will begin to torture this Ego by inflicting upon him new ones. If it may be said that there is not a mental or physical suffering in the life of a mortal which is not the direct fruit and consequence of some sin in a preceding existence; on the other hand, since he does not preserve the slightest recollection of it in his actual life, and feels himself not deserving of such punishment, and therefore thinks he suffers for no guilt of his own, this alone is sufficient to entitle the human soul to the fullest consolation, rest, and bliss in his *post-mortem* existence. Death comes to our spiritual selves ever as a deliverer and friend. For the materialist, who, notwithstanding his materialism, was not a bad man, the interval between the two lives will be like the unbroken and placid sleep of a child, either entirely dreamless, or filled with pictures of which he will have no definite perception; while for the average mortal it will be a dream as vivid as life, and full of realistic bliss and visions.

ENQ. Then the personal man must always go on suffering *blindly* the Karmic penalties which the Ego has incurred?

THEO. Not quite so. At the solemn moment of death every man, even when death is sudden, sees the whole of his past life marshalled before him, in its minutest details. For one short instant the *personal* becomes one with the *individual* and all-knowing *Ego*. But this instant is enough to show to him the whole chain of causes which have been at work during his life. He sees and now understands himself as he is, unadorned by flattery or self-deception. He reads his life, remaining as a spectator looking down into the arena he is quitting; he feels and knows the justice of all the suffering that has overtaken him.

ENQ. Does this happen to everyone?

THEO. Without any exception. Very good and holy men see, we are taught, not only the life they are living, but even several preceding lives in which were produced the causes that made them what they were in the life just closing. They recognize the law of Karma in all its majesty and justice.[12]

****

... This Law [of Retribution]—whether Conscious or Unconscious—predestines nothing and no one. It exists from and in Eternity, truly, for it is Eternity itself; and as such, since no act can be co-equal with eternity, it cannot be said to act, for it is Action itself. It is not the Wave which drowns a man, but the personal action of the wretch, who goes deliberately and places himself under the *impersonal* action of the laws that govern the Ocean's motion. Karma creates nothing, nor does it design. It is man who plans and creates causes, and Karmic law adjusts the effects; which adjustment is not an act, but universal harmony, tending ever to resume its original position, like a bough, which, bent down too forcibly, rebounds with corresponding vigour. If it happens to dislocate the arm that tried to bend it out of its natural position, shall we say that it is the bough which broke our arm, or that our own folly has brought us to grief? Karma has never sought to destroy intellectual and individual liberty, like the God invented by the Monotheists. It has not involved its decrees in darkness purposely to perplex man; nor shall it punish him who dares to scrutinize its mysteries. On the contrary, he who unveils through study and meditation its intricate paths, and throws light on those dark ways, in the windings of which so many men perish owing to their ignorance of the labyrinth of life, is working for the good of his fellow-men. Karma is an Absolute and Eternal law in the World of manifestation; and as there can only be one Absolute, as One eternal ever present Cause, believers in Karma cannot be regarded as Atheists or materialists—still less as fatalists: for Karma is one with the Unknowable, of which it is an aspect in its effects in the phenomenal world.

Intimately, or rather indissolubly, connected with Karma, then, is the law of re-birth, or of the reincarnation of the same spiritual individually in a long, almost interminable, series of personalities.[13]

****

. . . Ever turn away your gaze from the imperfections of your neighbour and centre rather your attention upon your own short-comings in order to correct them and become wiser. . . . Show not the disparity between claim and action in another man but——whether he be brother or neighbour—rather help him in his arduous walk in life . . . The problem of true theosophy and its great mission is the working out of clear, unequivocal conceptions of ethic ideas and duties which would satisfy most and best the

altruistic and right feeling in us; and the modelling of
these conceptions for their adaption into such forms
of daily life where they may be applied with most
equitableness. . . . Such is the common work in view
for all who are willing to act on these principles. It is a
laborious task and will require strenuous and perse-
vering exertion, but it must lead you insensibly to
progress and leave no room for any selfish aspirations outside the limits traced. . . . .[14]

References

[1] H. P. Blavatsky, *The Key to Theosophy*, London and New York: The
Theosophical Publishing Society, 1889.

[2] The Theosophical Glossary, London: The Theosophical Publishing Society, 1892.

[3] *The Theosophist*, Adyar, Vol. V, No. 9, June 1884, p. 223; *H. P. Blavatsky
Collected Writings*, Ed. by Boris de Zirkoff, Vol. VI, p. 237.

[4] "Morality and Pantheism," *The Theosophist*, Vol. V, No. 2, Nov. 1883, pp.
33-34; *Collected Writings*, Vol. V, p. 335.

[5] *The Secret Doctrine*, orig. ed., Vol. II, p. 420.

[6] Ibid., Vol. II, p. 302 fn.

[7] Ibid., Vol. II, p. 303.

[8] Blavatsky, *Key*, pp. 135-142.

[9] Ibid., pp. 201-207

[10] Ibid., pp. 46-47.

[11] "Faith in Astrology," *The Theosophist*, Vol. VI, No. 5, February 1885, p.
106; *Collected Writings*, Vol. VI, p. 327.

[12] Blavatsky, *Key*, pp. 161-162.

[13] Blavatsky, *The Secret Doctrine*, Vol. II, pp. 304, 306.

[14] "Original Programme" Manuscript, Ostende, Oct. 3rd, 1886; *Collected
Writings*, Vol. VII, p. 170.

H.P. BLAVATSKY BIBLIOGRAPHY

The Collected Writings, Volumes I through XI, 1874-1889, compiled by Boris de Zirkoff. The Theosophical Publishing House,
Adyar, London, Wheaton (Illinois). Other volumes in progress.

The Key to Theosophy. Original edition: The Theosophical Publishing Society, London and New York, 1889; many subsequent
editions.

The Secret Doctrine. Original edition in two volumes, The
Theosophical Publishing Co., London, New York and Adyar,
1888; many subsequent editions. 6th edition in six volumes,
The Theosophical Publishing House, Adyar, 1971.

The Theosophical Glossary. The Theosophical Publishing Society,
London, 1892; several subsequent editions.

2.

The Rhythmic Return
To Equilibrium

JAMES S. PERKINS

In Ancient Egypt artists created statues and paintings of the Gods with the intent that the Gods should enter and reside in their creations. Hence works of art became sacred objects. Since the Gods were supermundane beings, obedient to cosmic law, any human artists who would represent them had to be cognizant of those imperatives of all true creation, the universal principles, among which are unity, balance, proportion, rhythm, and harmony. These eternals are observed to be actively present in Nature and were known to philosophers and high priests as composing the very foundations of universal order. Special attention was given by the Egyptian artists to balance and symmetrical harmony, which is evident in their constant return to the squared order in their designs, beginning with the design of the pyramids.

To modern students, also, who are interested in the occult aspects of Nature, these principles are of fundamental importance. It is now widely understood that the whole of creation is a progressive unfoldment of Absolute Motion, motion that is cyclic, the impulses of which generate their own return to equilibrium. From the beginning of time, and throughout the evolving movement, this cyclic action and reaction has been ceaseless. The original, primeval impulse, being omnipotent, gave rise to the infinite concatenations of cycles within cycles in ever denser matter, resulting in the multilevel universe as we know it. Within it, all motion is ever seeking to return to balance. At every level, physical, emotional, mental, and spiritual, any cycle's restoration of equilibrium releases its energies into yet greater cycles that are themselves returning to some more inclusive equilibrium, a procedure that leads ultimately to supreme harmony, the end purpose of the universe.

So viewed, the entire cosmic process is simply a movement from an original state of equipoise into creative motion and return to equilibrium. This lawful motion has been noted in various ways in ancient cultures in terms having the equivalent meaning that the word *Karma* has for us today, namely the law of action and reaction. Throughout the ages various interpreters of the law have adapted its meaning to religious creeds and beliefs, particularly in fields of morality and spiritual beneficence, or the reverse. Every enduring religion and philosophy must deal with the distinction between good and evil. The ethical, moral, and spiritual mores, as determined by each religion's ultimate authority, have gained validity insofar as they have embodied or expressed universal principles. In all religions we see in their pronouncements of right and wrong the law of Karma incorporated in one way or another. Further, since the cyclic nature of Karma also invites predictive discernment, this aspect, too, has been employed in prognosticating good and ill fortune. All by-paths stemming from the main highway of true spiritual knowledge beget endless fears, forebodings, and anxieties. The Karma-nemesis of the Greeks, for example, conveyed an ominous foreshadowing of dark furies descending, remindful of certain religious ideas of avenging angels, and the designations of divine wrath upon unrepentant violators of the Law as proclaimed.

An enlightened Occult Science must restore the concept of Karma to its more accurate meaning as an immutable principle in Nature—the principle of balance—that acts eternally and everywhere to return the cycles of action in worlds of matter, as well as of emotions, mind, and spirit, to an equilibrium of universal harmony. Karma neither rewards nor punishes. It is a law that brings every action to its right adjustment, a law that can be used beneficially in all of life's situations; but through human ignorance it is a law that more often than not operates to cause suffering, sorrow and destruction.

Divorced from the element of superstition, Karma may be more truly conceived, perhaps, in a modern terminology as the "feed-back" system of the functioning universe; it automatically rectifies inefficient or disharmonious use of the machinery of existence. Man is self-generator of innumerable thought-patterns and desire-impulses, followed by physical acts, each of which becomes a circuit of forces that can be closed only by the reaction that has been generated. We write our own tickets to glory and gloom. Usually our thinking centers mistakenly upon the idea that if we can close the door against threatened adversity, or open some promising window of opportunity, all main problems will disappear. Yet the "karmic mice" materialize out of the very walls to harass us with fresh concerns. No force can break the Divine Order. But as in all arts, so in the art of living, knowledge makes possible a more skillful use of the rectifying law by diligently applying Nature's eternal principles to all mundane existence.

We might view these principles in a natural order of obtainment. If we assume that thee is One Source of all life, and given the Absolute Motion of creation, the principle of *unity* is then primary. Universal *order* appears when the Absolute Motion is perceived in its cyclic measurements, numbers, and proportions. *Rhythm* becomes manifest with the repetitive cycles of motion.

Balance is the unfailing closure of every cycle. *Harmony* proceeds from balance, and is dependent upon it, harmony being what occurs when balance is achieved, namely a momentary alignment with the Source of Life that reveals some new face of Truth. Through harmony every living thing in Nature is flashing its meaning in the total scheme of life. This ceaseless "information service" can be considered therefore among the universal principles, and might naturally be termed *revelation*.

Given the preceding six principles, a seventh appears as the culmination of universal purpose. Innate in all evolving life, is the eternal attraction toward attainment of archetypal perfection. This will-to-perfection is imperative in evolution, having been ceaselessly active throughout the universe from the beginning. It provides the orientation that guides Nature in the slow evolution of all forms and species toward their fulfillment. In man's consciousness, too, this principle is ever operative. The instinct to progress to a better state of affairs, or a more ideal situation, is more than a human hope; it is an urge rooted in the primeval purpose of life. It may be inactive at times but is constantly present and ready, when stimulated, to awaken fresh motivation. We see Man, despite all frustration and denial, ever responding to newborn purpose, a new day, a new age, with new hope eternally springing in his breast—all of which testifies to an obligatory impellent latent in him, as well as in every other living thing, to achieve the perfect state. This universal attraction is viewed here as a seventh principle in Nature—*perfection*.

With these seven principles listed as above, it may be noted that balance is in the central position. Harmony is subsequent to balance. Balance is essential to any manifestation of harmony. There cannot be harmony without balance. This sequence becomes significant when we recall what one of the greatest Adepts in the spiritual sciences has stated, "We recognize but one law in the universe, the law of harmony."[1] Why did he not refer to Karma as the fundamental law? Coming from such a source, the statement alerts one's attention. Why would harmony be singled out as paramount to Karma, or even to unity?

It is true that harmony is the vesture and expression of universal love bringing all forces and forms into true alignment with their cosmic source. Harmony achieved in any creative action renders beautiful with love what is taking place inexorably through the law of balance. Harmony and balance seem to be interwoven, with harmony as the supreme possibility, the crowning attainment that is innate in the action of the law of balance. But harmony awaits the successful employment of balance. A bridge, beautifully designed, may be a harmony and unity of lines and masses on paper, but the actual structure will collapse if the elements that uphold it do not at all times balance the forces bearing upon it. Harmony and unity disappear in the resulting crash. But the principle of balance is instantly reasserted in the bridge's segments lying scattered on the ground, each equilibrized by forces of gravity and inertia. Harmony was not achieved because the principle of balance was not employed successfully. This sequential order of balance and then harmony is again clearly exemplified in any true work of art. A proportionate balance of all the necessary elements has to be properly assembled and arranged prior to the appearance of a harmony of the whole. Harmony, as said, adds to balance the element of love, which makes manifest the reality of unity and beauty. The law of Karma brings all cyclic action back to equilibrium, but how we behave in this action, what we do creatively with love to render it harmonious, is the supreme value in the experience. Harmony is as a divine chariot drawn by the horses of balance and all the other principles. Viewed similarly, perhaps one might think of harmony as the supreme law in the universe.

The enrichment that can come into our lives through a knowledgeable employment of the law of Karma is limitless. Although Karma functions inexorably, as does the law of gravitation, both laws are equally usable for creative and beneficial purposes. It requires hardly more than mere awareness of this law to awaken an appreciable measure of spiritual self-reliance, a virtue that today seems to be disappearing phenomenally, even among advocates of the spiritual life.

With deeper consideration of the universal law that tells us in simplest terms that we will reap what we sow, we are faced with taking into account those larger cycles of reaping that could only have been "sown" in some other time prior to the present lifetime. Clearly, some of our actions that occur under extraordinary circumstances, and which have crucial effect on other people and living things, will have repercussions for good or ill that extend beyond one's present span of life on earth.

A rhythm then, of recurring earth lives would be the most reasonable postulate for equilibrizing these more extensive cycles of adjustment. They would have to evolve through greater time-spans toward ultimate harmony. In fact, it seems that reincarnation is an irrefutable corollary of the cyclic law when applied to the more complex individual situations. Besides, in view of the other principles, a recurrence of earth lives is evidence in the human kingdom of the universal principle of rhythm. Recurrence would also render even more reasonable and evident the principles of harmony, revelation and perfection.

Clear thinking seems to compel us to expand the horizon of life's duration beyond the confining barriers of the birth and death of our present physical body. The more profoundly one realizes the human situation, the more certainly he sees that Reincarnation and Karma are indissolubly linked as though they were the two sides of a single coin. It follows from such a conclusion that man is a being of far greater potentials than he is likely to imagine—a conclusion that calls for recognition of an immortal element in his being. The recognition goes further, in fact, to that of viewing the immortal element as the *Real Self* in man. With this awareness becoming a reality, the path to supreme knowledge lies immediately ahead.

The beginning of wonder in this direction and the accompanying "love of lonely study" are initial stages in a more rapid growth of the soul, and the beginning of man's true enlightenment. For, as Sri Shankaracharya assures us, it is through soul-knowledge alone that the universe shall be known—the universe both visible and invisible. Overriding all is the law of Karma, the principle of balance. From the soul's point of view Karma is a liberating agent because it functions infallibly to return the true fruit of every seed that is sown. Therefore by remote control this law guarantees that man, when he awakens, can be master of his destiny. One may choose a higher path today with very little apparent effect upon the events of his life. However, if he is a true perceiver of the law, there is not only knowledge of, but a growing faith in, its working. Where there is to be any change in life's course the momentum of the previous course has to be overcome. This is where faith in the law must become the factor of safety if the new course is to be pursued. In all of the great structures that man builds in this world, a factor of safety has to be calculated and continually accounted for in the planning. By analogy, if we may think of a successful employment of the law of Karma in structuring a new course of action for ourselves, the factor of safety to be kept active is faith in the law.

Many strange and dramatic instances might be introduced here to support the reality of this law's ceaseless functioning. But a proof that is universally available is at hand. We need only note the basic fears in man: first, the "normal" fear that through some ill fortune life will deprive him of what he has rightfully gained; and second, the fear of time's inevitable reduction through old age, or disaster, of his powers of adulthood and his position in life. The fear of loss of personal accumulations and of reduction to a lesser status of mortal existence testifies to a deeply ingrained uneasiness in us that inevitable justice is wrought for transgressions permitted in the past; and even for forgotten iniquities, inherited from some other time. These are natural fears that stem from the immortal soul's awareness—even though unrecognized by the person—of the action of Karmic law. Instinctively one knows that the progeny bred in all three worlds—mental, emotional, and physical—are attached to us and remain with us, having their growth to fulfillment and final demise via the cyclic law of action and reaction.

Yet this same law used creatively can bring release from such fears of want and loss. To know this positively is the beginning of freedom within the law, which is one of life's greater blessings. Karma works as truly for tapping the inexhaustible resources of the universe, as it does in the delightful balance of energies that unveil a rainbow in the sky. A great poet, who was also a Master of Life, could say with equanimity: "Clouds come floating into my life from other days, no longer to shed rain, or usher storm, but to give colour to my sunset sky."[2] A creative acceptance of life's patterns can grow out of an alert awareness of the eternally constructive purpose in the universe, as so beautifully worded by Sir Edwin Arnold: "Before beginning, and without an end, as space eternal and as surety sure, is fixed a Power Divine which moves to good, only its laws endure."[3]

If the night closes in upon my sunlit days, let me have faith that as surely as I now transform by will and thought the darkness into light within me, dawn will reappear outwardly, and the sunrise follow. It is not to prayers and penitence that I turn in my self-made prisons, but to action, employing the law. Deliverance is to be sought within. Our powers lie there, enticed forth by circumstances arising all about us. Life is the Teacher, yet if the teaching brings only growing strife and lusts, and hurt, succeeded by burdens of sorrow, how may the faded wheel of necessity be reversed? How other than by the creative usage of adversity? My soul is blessed by calamities to my person when these are made to be stepping stones, or wings to spread, aspiring to some happier abode in the Mystery Supreme.

Of all the advantages that a growing understanding of the law of Karma affords, this stirring towards self-transformation is the most rewarding. For it brings personal assurance that the principle of rhythmic return to equilibrium—Karma—will unfold in time the manifestation of universal Harmony.

References

[1] *The Mahatma Letters to A.P. Sinnett,* transcribed and compiled by A.T. Barker, 3rd ed., Adyar: Theosophical Publishing House, 1962, Letter 22.

[2] Rabindranath Tagore.

[3] *The Light of Asia,* Sir Edwin Arnold.

3.

Karma and Reincarnation

L. H. LESLIE-SMITH

The themes of karma and reincarnation have been current and familiar in the East for many centuries. They have been progressively introduced into the West since the founding of The Theosophical Society in 1875 and have now permeated the thought of the world, at any rate as ideas. Whether accepted as hypotheses, beliefs, or possibilities, these subjects can be discussed in any assembly of intelligent persons. The thinking may be vague, for notions will commonly have been gathered from novels, poems, and plays rather than from any considered presentation. But such media have proved excellent for putting forward fresh or unorthodox concepts. Whereas a well prepared and reasoned statement is apt to be rejected out of hand as at variance with conventional thought and belief, the same ideas in the form of entertainment, or in a cultural setting, raise no automatic barriers. The ordinary reactive defenses are bypassed because the challenge is not made in real life but in a kind of fantasy world of the arts.

Obviously, belief has nothing to do with fact. The disbelief of the majority of men cannot make a truth false; and an untrue statement is rendered none the less so because the whole world believes it to be correct. Nor can our earnest desire that something may be true affect its validity in the least. Further, it is no use trying to fit facts into some theory. We must seek a postulate that is not only warranted by the facts but is also a reasonable theory that explains things previously obscure. Thus, though half the peoples of the earth believe in reincarnation, that in itself is no reason for accepting the doctrine, but only for carefully examining it, the evidence for it, and its rationale, in order to form our own opinion. This investigation must be done objectively, with a mind free from bias and preconception and an attitude of openness and receptivity, yet with the critical faculty fully alert. Both karma and reincarnation are vast subjects in their complex application, but their general principles are easy to understand. Let us look at them briefly.

That the universe runs according to law has been axiomatic in theosophical thought, and this is now widely accepted in modern thinking. Every discovery of science seems to confirm it so far as the physical world is concerned. Only on such a basis could technologists have achieved the superb feat of putting men on the moon. H. P. Blavatsky said, "Deity is Law and vice-versa." So-called miraculous occurrences are due to the operation or use of some law, within the all-embracing law of nature, of which we are mostly yet ignorant. Enough "miracles" have been performed by physical means in this century to make this clear. Few people, however, have applied this principle to the more subtle psychic realms. Yet when a law is found working at one level of existence, one can be sure that it works correspondingly at all other levels, though seemingly different, perhaps, because operating in other circumstances and conditions. The whole of nature is one, a unity. "As above, so below" is an occult maxim, which is equally true the other way around. Law is fundamental to all existence.

The most important aspect of universal law, according to H. P. Blavatsky, is the law of adjustment, of balance, of causation, called karma. She calls it "the *Ultimate Law* of the Universe, the source, origin and fount of all the laws which exist throughout Nature. Karma is the unerring law which adjusts effect to cause on the physical, mental and spiritual planes of being." Whenever and wherever imbalance is produced, the self-adjusting intelligent "mechanism" comes into play to restore equilibrium. The root meaning of karma is action; hence it applies to the whole of nature, including man, for action is involved in all manifestation.

It is somewhat confusing that the same word is used for the relation of cause to effect in the lower kingdoms of nature as for humanity, where alone "whatsoever a man soweth, that shall he also reap." Karma not only keeps the stars on their courses and every atom in being, but it also adjusts moral relationships resulting from the power of choice, which is one of the distinguishing characteristics of man. H. P. B. gives the difference when she says that karma is the "law of adjustment which ever tends to restore disturbed equilibrium in the physical and broken harmony in the moral world." To A. P. Sinnett, karma was "the law of ethical causation," which would restrict it to the human race; in that context it seems a fair definition. Repeatedly, H. P. B. speaks of the law of retribution. To modern ears this suggests vengeance, but formerly the word included the meaning of compensation or recompense. Having moral significance, this also can apply to human beings.

The doctrine of karma is nowhere more clearly and yet more profoundly expounded than in *The Key to Theosophy*, by H. P. Blavatsky, from which the quotations given above and those to follow are taken unless otherwise stated. Universally, "Karma is that unseen and unknown law *which adjusts wisely, intelligently and equitably* each effect to its cause." Humanly, "Karma gives back to every man the actual consequences of his own action." It follows that it is "an unfailing redresser of human injustice; a stern adjuster of wrongs; a retributive law which punishes and rewards with equal impartiality. It is no respecter of persons" and it "can neither be propitiated nor turned aside by prayer." Inexorably thus it achieves not only the Mikado's sublime object of letting "the punishment fit the crime"; it also complements it justly by making the reward fit the merit. We have to take responsibility for our own actions; the law will surely return results to us. The small boy's plea, "He told me to do it," is no excuse; nor is an order from one in authority or that other common plaint, "I didn't mean to do it." Motive indeed is important and must mitigate the moral force of any action, though it cannot affect the physical result.

The general principle is simple. "It does not require metaphysics or education to make a man understand the broad truths of Karma and Reincarnation." It is one of the splendid features of the theosophical philosophy that the general outline can be easily grasped; yet the greatest minds cannot fully comprehend the implications and ramifications. One is apt to think that one knows about karma. But it is not much that one knows.

Since no person can live to himself and is inevitably caught up in human relationships, the application of karma is bound to be complex. For "the aggregate of individual Karma becomes that of the nation to which those individuals belong, and the sum of national Karma is that of the world." And again, "The interdependence of humanity is the cause of what is called Distributive Karma, and it is this law which affords the solution to the great question of collective suffering and its relief." The individual karma of every man and woman is inextricably linked with that of the group, and through the group with the entire human race.

"Karma is the force that impels to Reincarnation, and that Karma is the destiny man weaves for himself." In any one life we sow the seeds of the personality of the next incarnation. That is the hypothesis. Reincarnation is the method by which human karma, at any rate, works. The two are inseparably interwoven.

This concept offers greater understanding of our
lives and of those of the people around us. The circumstances that make things easy for some, hard for others,
and well-nigh impossible for still others, are karmic-
—the precise outcome of their own behavior in the past.
That, however, is no reason for not giving anyone all
the help we can. Indeed, not to do so would be to build
an appropriate failure into our future, in this incarnation or another. That is why today is of the utmost
importance; not only today, but this hour, this minute,
for by what we do this very moment, every present
moment, we mold our tomorrow.

The interdependence of mankind involves group
and national karma. We are all intimately linked both
with the cultural group into which we are born and with
the race or nation of which that group is part. Karma of
our own making placed us in the setting of a mystique
that is the cumulative result of the nation's history—an
aura or mental-emotional atmosphere created by untold generations of our forefathers. This brings in distributive karma, by which the doings of a group involve
all members of that group, whether or not they approve
of them. This could possibly explain the statement that
after death the Ego (the reincarnating individuality, not
the personality, which modern psychology calls the
"ego") receives only "the reward for the unmerited
suffering endured during its past incarnation." At any
rate, just as none can avoid the results of his own actions, so oone can stay or turn aside the karma of his
group. One cannot run away and opt out of it. If its
problems are not faced now, one will remain tied to
them karmically in future lives, in future nations
perhaps, until proper balance is restored. This raises
interesting and cogent points. Is the minority that de-
serts its native land to settle elsewhere a band of heroes
or a bunch of escapists? This question becomes more
fascinating in the case of those emigrants who in their

new world persecuted those who disagreed with them as fiercely as they themselves had been persecuted before they left their homeland.

Karmic forces return to their individual originators; but with the intricate network in any group they would seem likely to meet and be affected by other forces. The result would thus be a modification of the original. Karmic debts have to be paid. Yet, like ordinary ones, may they not sometimes be met by an altruistic benefactor? Can this not also be within the province of distributive karma? H. P. B. says that "no man can rise superior to his individual failings without lifting, be it ever so little, the whole body of which he is an integral part." Thus he eases a little of the "heavy karma of the world," as it has been put, for his fellows and thereby may be said to a small extent to redeem them. Is not this, raised to a superlative degree, what those great men have done who have been called the saviors of mankind?

All students of Theosophy are familiar with a further aspect of universal law: the law of cycles or of periodicity. This is self-evident in nature—ebb and flow, night and day, waking and sleeping, and so on. A period of activity and growth is followed by one of assimilation and rest. Reincarnation is another example of the same process. After death, Devachan. But death is not just the dissolution of the physical body. That is said to be followed by a widely varied period during which base desires are worked out and purged. The successive breaking up of the lower aspects of the personality culminates in the "second death," which marks the end of that mortal personality. All its spiritual aspirations and higher qualities—"eternal qualities such as love and mercy"—are transferred to the Ego. The complex of body, emotions, brain, of each of us, answering to a certain name, will vanish and its various constituents be resolved again into the matter of their respective planes—"dust to dust" at the physical level, and so forth. "Personal consciousness can hardly last longer than the personality itself." Hence a personality can win relative immortality only by rejecting its lower life of personal desire for one of devotion to unselfish service, whose spiritual qualities can be absorbed by the Ego.

Successive personalities are likened to parts in a series of dramas—or comedies—played by the same actor, the reincarnating individuality. This Ego "retains during the Devachanic period merely the essence of the experience of its past earth life or personality"; but "all that constituted during life the *spiritual* bundle of experiences, the noblest aspirations and *unselfish* nature, clings for the time of the Devachanic period of the Ego. The *actor* is so imbued with the role just played that he dreams of it during the whole Devachanic night." So, "collecting from every terrestrial personality, into which Karma forces it to incarnate, the nectar alone of the spiritual qualities and self-consciousness, it unites all these into one whole and emerges from its chrysalis as the glorified Dhyan Chohan. So much the worse for the personalities from which it could collect nothing. Such personalities cannot assuredly outlive consciously their terrestrial existence."

The karmic connection between lives is made by *skandhas*, bundles of attributes. These are psychomental link mechanisms by which characteristics are passed from one personality to its successors. They correspond to the DNA, gene, chromosome arrangement of inherited qualities in the physical bodies. They are, as it were, the seeds of character, representing innate faculty and capability—or lack of it. At death they "remain as karmic effects, as germs, in the atmosphere of the terrestrial plane to attach themselves to the new personality of the Ego when it reincarnates."

What of Devachan? "Devachan is a state of mental bliss . . . analogous to but far more vivid and real than the most vivid dream." It is an idealistic and subjective continuation of earth life, a dream world of our own fashioning. The world of this present life is also the creation of our own minds through sense impressions made on the brain—also an illusion, we are told. After the death of Keats, Shelley wrote: "He hath awakened from the dream of life." Are both this life and the post-mortem one simply dreams, seemingly very real, one more highly colored than the other? Again, H. P. B. said "Death is sleep." What relation have sleep and dreams to Reality? These are questions worth pondering. Maybe our concepts need looking at again. We can accept without reservation the validity of the cyclic law, but we may well be cautious with interpretations of its application on the various planes of being and guard against the tendency to fixed ideas.

"The period between births is said to extend to ten to fifteen centuries." *The Mahatma Letters to A. P. Sinnett*, however, gives a hundred times longer "in the transitory sphere of *effects* than on the globes." Was 1,500 reckoned to be a hundred times the average length of life in those days—fifteen years, owing to the high mortality rate in infancy? There is this also: "In eternity the longest periods of time are as the wink of an eye." Then surely a seeming period of fifteen centuries might actually pass in a few minutes, hours, days, weeks. There is no common time scale, and comparisons could easily lead us astray in our thinking. Maybe in meditation sometime a flash of illumination and understanding will come.

The theories, hypotheses, doctrines—as suits us best—of karma and reincarnation present a scheme of law that can throw light on evolution and can make some sense of life and death, rendering the former intelligible and the latter negligible. They show a pattern that explains the world as it is with its many human problems. They offer a unique philosophy for living and an unrivaled basis for moral values.

Human potentialities unfold slowly yet surely under the law of adjustment, which is wholly educative, teaching men by experience until they come to realize their responsibility, not only to their fellows but also to the other kingdoms of nature. Only what is worthy of the immortal center within each one of us can survive. All the separative qualities—pride, possessiveness, selfishness—have to go. By stripping away these, by discarding the illusory toys on which the world sets great store, a man may return to his native purity of soul, through which divine light and wisdom may be manifested in a human being.

The modern crs is for man to take charge of his destiny. Unconsciously he has always been responsible, for present actions mold his future, just as his own past actions have predestined the present. But if we are consciously to shape the future—a task that evolution is steadily forcing on us—then only a knowledge of the great laws of karma and reincarnation can enable us to do so wisely.

4.

The Source of Becauses

CLARENCE R. PEDERSEN

"All things have 'becauses,' " wrote Arthur Koestler in his book, *Act of Creation*,[1] in what may be the most succinct explanation of the *modus operandi* of nature ever offered by a philosopher. For of the many questions which puzzle the mind of man, the concept of karma as cause and effect, or action and reaction, has long been one of the most challenging and disturbing. Throughout history this concept has been debated, described, deified, and denied. It has been the basis of much philosophical theory, religious dogma, and scientific deduction. The ontologist finds this aspect of nature intrinsic to life, for ontology becomes a meaningless science unless karma is incorporated as one of the fundamental aspects of being. Sociologically, karma, even when unrecognized as such has been the rationale behind our concept of justice.

To those who have studied reincarnation as a doctrine essential to the theory of evolution, karma is a most meaningful concept. Regarding karma as action plus the results of action, the student recognizes that the proper consideration of events cannot be complete unless the preceding related activity, plus the sequel to an event, then the sequel to the sequel, *ad infinitum*, are all considered as integral parts of the entire chain of action.

Defining karma in *The Secret Doctrine*,[2] H. P. Blavatsky wrote: "Karma ... is eternity itself; and as such, since no act can be co-equal with ETERNITY, it cannot be said to act, for it is ACTION itself." It would seem from this definition that karma must have come into operation with the first instant of manifestation, the first instant of creation. For manifestation is action; in addition, it automatically establishes a dichotomy between the source of the creation and the created, a bifurcation which is, so to speak, the very "nature of nature." Thus there is this act of separation which might be termed "First Cause."

According to the theosophical philosophy, it was from this original act of creation that vast numbers of microcosmic units of consciousness, all deriving from the Absolute Principle, began their evolution. Each of these units, being essentially a spark of the Divine, became a microcosmic world in itself, each able to create in its own right by projecting portions of itself into the world outside. It is suggested that as the act of creation by Deity is the beginning of macrocosmic karma, so the first reaching out of the individual soul is the beginning of karma at the microcosmic level. Here too, although on an infinitely smaller scale, there is the creator and the created, with action as the relationship between them. It is implied, of course, that at the earliest stage of evolution, the mental capacities of the units of consciousness are still latent, and thus no personal responsibility is attached to action. In this highly undifferentiated state, karma is simply physical cause and effect, involving groups of dimly conscious units.

Nevertheless, because the superficial diversity of these sparks of consciousness leads to a vast assortment of conflicting creativity, and because the unpolarized noumenon always resists the establishment of polarized phenomena, we find that the projection of consciousness creates an "unnatural" tension, an imbalance within the universe. We note an incessant tug of war throughout creation, first a pulling away from the center of being (centrifugal force), then a compensatory reaction, a pulling back to the center (centripetal force). This rubber band-like quality of nature eliminates imbalance and restores the universal ethic of harmony.

We find further that within the localization of each unit of consciousness, as the personality moves from a state of latency, there is the development of a subjective dichotomy due to the relatedness between various components of the pscyhe. Here also nature strives to overcome the resulting disharmony.

Thus we find that the act of creation is basically divisive, but that nature, the moment it creates this diversity, immediately demands the reunion of the separate parts.

We may say that there appears to be within nature an exquisite tendency toward maintaining the status quo of pure spirit—spirit unsullied and unencumbered by the matter of manifestation. God, we may say, observing what he has wrought, immediately repents his rashness. Unable to recall that portion of his consciousness which he has willed forth, he now does the next best thing and proceeds to negate the effects of First Cause. It is, then, this need to eliminate polarity which seems to be the "cause" of cause and effect. This is an underlying quality of nature, and its manifested result is the law of compensation.

There have of course been many different interpretations of karma and how it affects life. As with all laws which operate in realms not susceptible to empirical evidence, the various conclusions reached concerning karma have been conditioned by the limited nature of man's knowledge and by his desire to adjust his philosophy to meet his needs and inclinations. Under these limitations, complete objectivity of interpretation is impossible, and so we find that karma frequently means different things to different people.

For instance, many people believe that karmic law is

based upon an ethical interpretation of action—that the
nature of reaction is dependent upon an evaluation of
action in relation to certain ethical standards. As these
standards vary with the psychological uniqueness of the
individual, they cannot be designated as universal
moral imperatives, and it would therefore be inaccurate
to interpret karma on this basis.

The belief in karma as an evaluator of the ethics of
human behavior has at times led to the conclusion that
karmic reaction is instigated by a force or forces ex-
traneous to the perpetrator of the action. Such a conclusion is not surprising if we consider the background
of many major religions. Here we find that command-
ments for ethical behavior have traditonally been
"given" to man by Deity. Therefore, karma, accepted in
this sense, has also assumed the status of divinity. We
find, in the Hindu religion, that the *Lipika* (Lords of
Karma) have become the personal karmic administrators in the same way that Jehovah, the God of the
Jews, Gentiles, and Moslems, has been personalized as a
stern but just God. As an evaluator of ethics, karma has
become a guarantee of justice, *as justice is understood from
the point of view of the personality;* consequently it has
become a concept restricted by the limits of the human
psyche.

However, as all action is related either directly or
indirectly to First Cause, and as it appears that the
nature of the primordial Source reflects an inherent
need to expand creativity through the unfoldment of its
basic integrative nature, it would appear that action
which deviates from this original impulse would be
subject to corrective influences. Thus, any action which
tends to hurt or dwarf life might be considered unethi-
cal, and the reaction might tend to redirect the drive of
the actor.

But, if karma is truly the need of the Creator to dispel
the polarity of manifestation, this need must perforce

apply to *all* activity, and thus it would seem that morality would not be a necessary factor. In this sense, karma would simply be the agent which in effect nullified all action by means of reaction.

One effect of (or reaction to) this ethical interpretation of karma has sometimes been a fear of acting because of the consequences which might follow. Thus we find the development within some people of an inclination toward noninvolvement in the human scene, toward abstinence from action. This manifests in many cases as a strong tendency to live what might be called a "karmaless" existence. This situation might possibly be compared to the germination of a physical antibody, an attempt to instill within the psyche an antikarma serum composed of anti-emotional matter, which manifests as a strong desire to repress activity.

Now if we accept the fact that part of the reason for physical incarnation is objective experiencing through relationship, it appears that such a nihilistic approach to life would be contrary to our basic will to act. It seems that life, to fulfill its *dharma* (purpose), must include both subjective and objective activity, the degree of each depending upon the stage of development of the individual Ego.* Thus, inordinate deliberate withdrawal from life would seem to be in opposition to the natural unfoldment of man's consciousness. In other words, man's greatest "sin" might be an attempt to avoid his karma; the attempt by the personality to achieve morality by becoming amoral. Such an attempt to circumvent natural law cannot succeed, of course, for an "attempt" implies action to which there would be a reaction. The karma which would follow this negative approach to life would seem to be in the nature of emotional distortion of the psyche; the result might be that, in the future, before engaging in the normal activity of living, the

*Understood here as the true identity, the reincarnating entity, rather than the ego as identified in modern psychology.

personality would have to overcome the tendency to repress action. This "need to overcome" would be the karma of the Ego and would presumably manifest in the psyche as a specific attribute based on fear.

"Karma," wrote Arthur Robson in his book, *Look at Your Karma,*[3] "means 'actions,' 'doing,' but is used of those things only that we do by natural impulse, innate tendency. In other words one's karma is the sum of one's habits, tendencies, mannerisms and peculiarities of nature, as manifested in what one does."

According to this definition, it would seem that karma proceeds invariably from the psychic force field of the "doer" and never from the occasion itself; that for the occasion to be reactive, to be an effect of a cause previously traced to the "doer," there must be an active acceptance of the occasion by the "doer," whether this acceptance be positive or negative.

Karma in this sense is simply doing and redoing by the unit of consciousness and makes consciousness synonymous with action. In no way does it imply a reaction by the "not-I." Thus, events emanating from the "not-I" cannot be considered as retributive, edifying, or rewarding in themselves. Rather, their effects upon the psyche depend upon the manner of acceptance by the psyche, and this acceptance is subject to the amplifications or modifications of the will of the center of consciousness.

Examining our concept from this point of view, it might be helpful to divide the consideration of karma into three categories: the karma of anticipation; the karma of realization; the karma of remembrance. This last is, of course, a correlative of the first but is used here in the sense of regretting or enjoying a past activity. There is little room for debating the complete subjectivity of the first and third categories. Anticipation and remembrance of relationships with the "not-I" are qualities unique to each localization of consciousness. This leaves the karma of realization as the only type of karma which might be instigated by outside influences.

However, if we accept the fact that the Ego is autonomous within the limits of its psychic force field, that each unit of consciousness is a self-sustaining microcosm within the limits of macrocosmic law, then it seems logical to conclude that the unfoldment of consciousness is dependent upon the will of the Ego. The Ego is stimulated by outside energies only after it determines the need for a specific relationship and guides the consciousness correspondingly. Frequently such subjective motivation is generated from the deep layers of the unconscious, and thus may not be recognized by the waking consciousness.

Of course, Egoic action implies self-awareness but, as has been suggested, this condition is not manifest at the outset of creation.

Prior to what might be termed the "humanization" of the unit of consciousness, before the mental principle with its quality of reflection and judgment becomes manifest, there appear to be certain general guidelines arranged to direct the consciousness to an environment suitable for its evolutionary needs. Although karma, as action and reaction, is a factor in this "gestation period" of the Ego, there is as yet no self-awareness, and thus no basis for judging action in relation to development needs. Yet there is relative importance in this early activity, for the manner of acceptance by the consciousness of the original outside stimulus is the first transmutation of an attribute, a transmutation from a state of latency to one of manifested activity. The energies used in absorbing this experience will be converted into habit, so that subsequent experience will be correspondingly conditioned. Thus it seems that our first manner of accepting experience might be the most important, much as the training of an infant is more vital than that of later years.

It is suggested however that once consciousness has reached human status, the threads of the web of life are created solely by the Ego. Thereafter, at no time does any outside force penetrate within the "ring pass not" of the evolving consciousness. Indeed such an intrusion would seem to be contrary to the pattern of creation as understood by Theosophy, for inasmuch as the Ego bears complete responsibility for its actions, the will of the Ego, within the limits of natural law, must decide what relationships it should have.

Thus we find that karma is the web of life, the total pattern of cause and effect: causes originated by the Ego; effects depending upon the manner of acceptance by the Ego.

Granting the individual psyche this degree of autonomy helps to change our perspective of the influences of outside forces of human life. No longer will the "Lords of Karma"—a vaguely anthropomorphic group of superhumans—be our personal administrators; rather are we subject only to impersonal principle, to natural law. No longer will parochial morality be confused with the universal ethic. Rather, karma will tend to be accepted as a philosophy of complete self-responsibility, so complete that we ourselves must undertake any necessary corrective measures. We may see more clearly that each of us is a god unto himself; that we must not—nay, cannot—rely on outside circumstance to guide our evolution. For all necessary forces are available to each of us; being essentially divine, we can summon to our assistance the powers of divinity at any time we will. These powers of divinity are essential aspects of our own nature, not a part of life outside ourselves. As Dr. C. G. Jung remarks in his introduction to *The Tibetan Book of the Dead*, "The Soul [or, as here, the individual consciousness] is assuredly not small, but the radiant Godhead itself . . . even the gods are the radiance and reflections of our own souls. . . . The world of gods and spirits is truly 'nothing but' the collective unconscious inside me."[4]

From this it would seem that you as a person are the "doer," the creator of the occasion, or the responder to the occasion, or both. This of course means that there is never an event in the course of evolution which is in any way fortuitous or fatalistic. There is no arbitrariness in action. Purpose predominates. For karma, beginning with creation, will control creation until the time arrives for the Sound of Silence to return once more.

References

[1] Arthur Koestler, *Act of Creation*, New York: The Macmillan Co., 1964, p. 616.

[2] H. P. Blavatsky, *The Secret Doctrine*, Adyar: Theosophical Publishing House, 1938, vol. 3, p. 306.

[3] Arthur Robson, *Look at Your Karma*, Adyar: Vasanta Press, 1964. p. 2.

[4] W. Y. Evans-Wentz, *The Tibetan Book of the Dead*, New York: Oxford University Press, 1960. Introduction by C. G. Jung, pp. xxxix, li, lii.

5.

Karma and Cosmos

LAURENCE J. BENDIT
Part One

It is very easy to write or speak glibly about the doctrine of *Karma,* calling it the law of cause and effect, pithily stated in human terms by the Gospel saying that "Whatsoever a man soweth, that shall he also reap"; and so on. The statements are true. But in order to understand their deeper aspects we need to see the matter against a much wider background, that of the Cosmos itself. This Cosmos is a Whole, including everything from the very greatest to the most minute——remembering too that our own conception of great and small is limited by the horizons of our mental capacities, that is, the mind which perceives, at this present stage of the evolutionary pattern. This, in turn, means a mind only partly developed and operating, as a rule, far short of its latent capabilities.

Thus, before we come to karma itself, we should consider a few points relating to the universe we live in. To begin with, we need to see it as a single unit, in which anything occurring in any part of it influences, in however minute a degree, the rest. A person jumping on the earth, an electron shifting its orbit around an atomic nucleus, a star or galaxy exploding a thousand light-years away, sends a ripple of some kind throughout the physical universe. And, equally, a mental act of thought, feeling, perception, affects the whole of the psychic or mental and perhaps also the spiritual world.

This Whole, however, operates within its fields as if it

were subdivided—"granulated," to use Teilhard's phrase—into an infinite, or at least indefinite number of "monads." A monad can be defined, in line with both Leibnitz, H. P. Blavatsky, and others, as consisting of a nucleus within a field of matter or energies, contained by a "semipermeable membrane" or enclosing skin which at once connects it and separates it from its surroudings. Such a monad may be infinitely small (e.g. an electron) or on as vast a spatial scale as the universe itself. Typically, a single cell such as one of yeast shows us the basic monadic pattern: the nucleus is its creative center, holding the genetic material; the protoplasm is the surrounding field, while the outer membrane allows of a controlled circulation of material between the inner body of the cell and the fluid in which it lives.

In the *Stanzas of Dzyan,* the "skin" is called by the picturesque name of "the Ring Called Pass-Not" or, simply, the "Ring-Pass-Not." It is evident that each monad, great as a cluster of galaxies, small as an electron, is related to a hierarchy of other monads on its own scale or level; greater (as a cell is in an animal or vegetable body); or itself enclosing a number of smaller ones (atoms, molecules, etc.). On this pattern the Creation is built, or so it seems to us.

Before proceeding with our study it will be well if we establish firmly in the back of our minds that any such study can only present us with a relatively real picture of things. Owing to the limitations of our minds, we never see things as they are, but, at best, build up a picture more or less closely related to the actual truth. We do not see the truth itself. The importance of this will become apparent as we go on and it becomes clear that no understanding of our subject can arise until we are capable of combining at least two seemingly divergent forms of mental approach to it. In these the science of causality, which is our traditional Western mode of thinking, becomes wedded to another form of science, where synchronicity—the impact of events on the im-

mediate here and now—is the basis of another kind of
philosophy. The latter is mainly derived from Chinese
Taoism which, as it were, cuts at right-angles across the
linear, time-track habit of the West, adding a new di-
mension to our way of thinking. This gives a stereos-
copic view instead of one that is two-dimensional and
flat.

This can best be illustrated when we consider the
created and manifested universe which is our present
home, even from the level of the physical plane and
without going into the less defined and seemingly less
organized realm of the psyche or nonphysical. For
there are two schools of thought among cosmologists
today. One sees Creation as an Act (Latin: *Actus* or
Actum, something done and achieved) in time, hence as
having a beginning and an end. Indian thought tells of a
"Day of Brahma" or *Manvantara*, lasting so many mil-
lion years (presumably earth-years). This follows the
time-track and is in line with those modern astronomers
who see the universe beginning with a "big bang" and
gradually running down. But the other school, observing stars exploding, "black holes" appearing in outer
space, nebulae condensing into stars—and that within
our own lifetime—conceive the universe as in a state of
constant becoming: creation, destruction, re-creation
which might go on indefinitely. The latter tunes in with
the other kind of science, that of Taoism.

One is tempted to take sides, to accept one theory as
true, the other as false. But the occultist needs to develop the kind of mind which is able to see that both
approaches are true; since time is part of the *maya* or
self-created "illusion" by which we live, there is no fundamental contradiction between the synchronistic, Ta-
oist view and that of India and Western science. Together they can serve us in our search; one alone hides
Reality and gives us only a blinkered, partial view of
things-as-they-are, in truth.

So we can consider that what we call monads are in a constant state of being created, dissolved, and re-created all the time. They can be looked upon as existing off the line of time, as beginningless and endless, or as permanent entities. They exist, moreover, on every time scale, from the momentary one of certain sub-atomic particles to the apparent everlastingness of a galaxy, or, if not a galaxy, of the physical universe as a whole. The question is one of our ability to measure time with our mental processes. The same applies to the space-scale as between an electron and a cluster of stars. We do not know in any absolute way what either time or space may be. We know them only as we glimpse them at any NOW and HERE, in the "intersection of the timeless moment."

This, however, is to think only of the physical aspect of a monad, or of those monads which have physical existence. There is also the factor of consciousness, of the fullness or otherwise of the expression of the life within each one. We can, here, speak only in relation to man, the nearest kind of monadic unit to ourselves, and here we believe, rightly or wrongly, that on the evolutionary ladder we are the first to have the poten-tiality of self-identity, both of being a self-monad, and of knowing ourselves as self-monads. Who can say whether the center of a solar system or even a planet—what we call a god if not God—has anything like what we call a Self and is conscious of it-Self? It would be surprising if Selfhood were limited to such cosmic crea-tures as earth-men, but we do not know directly, even from the deepest mystical experience centering round our own selves; even if it shows us how much more there is beyond that Self, how much of the Divine remains unknown and unknowable so that it is called the Void and, equally aptly, the Plenum—the opposite of Void-ness.

I-ness is the center of man's Being, known in more

technical terms as the *Atman* operating through *Manas*, Pure Mind, within the "Ring-Pass-Not" of the physical body during physical incarnation. It is individual at root, yet one has to remember also that it is incorporated in the context of the Cosmos as a whole; it is made up of the same material as this Cosmos, planned on the same archetypal blueprint as every other monad, though the "protoplasmic" elements within its field will be differently arranged and will differ in their power as against one another, because of the individuality which is its nucleus. Moreover, these elements may, at any given time, operate in different patterns from their momentary and passing state outside the "Ring-Pass-Not" of an individuality: from what we call Nature, or the world outside us. This differential, however embryonic, in some measure alienates each of us from Nature and gives us a new relationship to that world. This in turn brings into being a certain stress, a field of force between the individual and "crude, unaided Nature" which, like any other energy field is at least potentially creative of new things.

This, at least in the definition I shall adopt, is where *karma* starts. No self, no karma. Introduce self and that self begins to interact actively with its environment, and that interaction is karma. There are some who speak of animals generating karma but, if this is the case, the term must be further extended to include all forms of action and reaction in any part of the universe. This is logical, but then the idea of karma is equated with the whole field of causality, even if this is entirely mechanical and devoid of any kind of consciousness or self-determination. It seems better to use the word in the narrower sense, as applied to the entity which has at least some degree of identity as a self. At the same time, such an idea has the value of making us realize the total integration of all levels of the world we live in, in terms of universally applicable law. The law of karma is, in the scientific sense, nothing but a "special case" within this universal law.

* * * * *

The idea of man being integral with the world in which he lives brings us to a most important consideration, which takes us back to our ideas on cosmology. Here we can find at least three languages in which we can start thinking thoughts about this universe, each of which embraces the seemingly conflicting pictures presented earlier.

First let us look at the statement made in a kind of shorthand in the *Stanzas of Dzyan*. These—said by H. P. Blavatsky to come from what may be the most ancient document in the world still in existence, hidden away in some remote library—are so obscure that either a highly developed intuition, or such immense commentaries as are contained in Blavatsky's major books are necessary to make them explicit.

We then have science where, at least as regards the physical world, vast progress has been made, especially since the day of Einstein. Surprisingly enough, this has resulted in showing us that matter is not really there at all, that at best something *may* be *somewhere in space at a particular moment of time*, but that is not so much certain as *probable*. (Incidentally, this discovery has brought some people back to a religious sense of the numinous which no amount of scriptural reading or theology could do. It has also brought into existence a new sacred language, that of Higher Mathematics, intelligible only to its initiates.)

More open to us, because closer to the ordinary mind, is the third approach, that which comes through the study of myth. Here we have a pantheon of beings supposedly immortal and superior to men. These equate with celestial bodies, stars, constellations, and planets, and also with various earth functions or features such as sky, sea, water, earth, and so on. In effect it would seem that when modern science speaks of energy, matter, spin, inertia, mass, gravity, speed, and so on, it really gives new names to the gods. These Gods (in the case of the Greeks especially) not only interfere in human affairs, but are often shown in conflict among themselves. In particular there is the strange idea of the displacement of the "Old Gods" by a new hierarchy, when the Titans, ruled by Kronos, were ousted by Kronos's upstart son, Zeus, and relegated to a remote sphere away from earth and its humanity: a story which can be taken to suggest the stresses and strains inevitable when a solar system breaks out of a galaxy, a planet from a central sun—and, it may be added, when a humanity or human monad becomes differentiated from the mass life of the biosphere and is individualized.

The relevance of this to the doctrine of karma is that man is made up of precisely the same "material"—i.e., forces and energies in one terminology, or of the very same gods in another—as the universe itself. In other words, the pantheon itself is not only outside him but also within. And, like the external world, it is active and dynamic at all levels from the physical "up" or "inward."

In the external world the gods may be said to be organized around a center which we call God. In man they cluster around the nucleus of Self, where they are governed by the same laws as govern the surrounding realms. But the effect of Self may be strong or weak, and so exerts more, or less, influence on the conflicting gods within its field; and conflicting they certainly are, until we learn how to bring them into order, which is the task of what we know as religion and its disciplines, simple or sophisticated.

Meanwhile, the personality which is made up of these forces interacts with its surroundings and generates karma. Our personal reaction to this is to find some effects pleasant and we call them good, or unpleasant, and we call them bad. In reality, karma is neither good nor bad; it is simply *karma* and is exactly suited to the causes which created it. Indeed, the working of the karmic law may be likened to that of a celestial computer. There is a tradition of certain Agencies known as the *Lipika* or Recording Angels. They do far more than keep ledgers of our acts. They are constantly being programmed with new information which, added to the material stored in their "memory" feeds back on this and alters the resulting impact from moment to moment. This result is in perfect dynamic balance from instant to instant. There is perfect justice throughout the whole universe.

* * * * *

All of this suggests that karma is a somewhat mechanistic process paralleled in Newton's famous law that "to every action there is an equal and opposite reaction." And so it is. Effect follows cause, inevitably. But it is obvious that in many cases a karmic reaction is not immediate, that many "wicked flourish like the green bay tree" and die in full enjoyment of the results of their misdeeds. But karma is not a fixed quantity like the debits or credits entered in an account book. It is made interestingly elastic because of the complexity of factors involved. We have not only the cyclic workings of the mechanical cosmos, we have other and more personal factors less mathematically exact to be placed along the time-track. One can forecast an eclipse or a certain stellar configuration, but one cannot accurately forecast what a living entity such as collective humanity, may do, and so what effects will result, let us say, at the time of some physical or meteorological event.

To a greater or less extent, the individual is involved in wars, revolutions, earthquakes so long as he is human: he seems to have no more free will or ability to choose his fate than the animal kingdom has to act of its own volition in the face of a cataclysmic storm or drought. But this is to forget that man, in addition to his involvement in the collective biosphere, is also a developing individual, within the "Ring-Pass-Not" of his personality. Moreover, unless the intuitions of the multitudes are only wishful thinking and not based on inner knowledge, it would seem that some form of man's individuality is not restricted to time. Following its own cycles, it returns to earth many times before it can become truly free of the "Wheel of Rebirth," after which it determines for itself whether or not it will make use of a new body.

In the meantime, the vast array of cosmic forces is working out its own pattern. In it the individual has his own unique place, and it may be that certain karmic forces do not come into manifest operation until the "slot" in time arrives into which that person fits. It is only as his inner Self takes charge of the personal field that a gradual growth of freedom of choice and will comes into view and modifies the resultant of karmic effects, at any given moment.

We should not think of karma as a fixed quantity so much as a constantly rebalancing and moving pattern impinging on an individual at each moment of time; and, further, that it is one in which individuality plays an increasing part.

This new turn of events is known both to psychologists and to all kinds of religious teachers or *gurus* as a stage in individual self-realization. It starts when the pupil or student comes consciously in touch with what I have called the pantheon within, begins to know "how he ticks," and brings the conflicting elements into harmony and order so that they work together instead of as a warring and self-negating mob.

Now, we may say, the processes of karma become reversed. In the past, the individual has been at their mercy, a more or less passive victim of his own acts.

Now, however, through what is taking place within him he becomes increasingly able to alter the effects of these past acts on his immediate situation. The gods within become harmonized, and no longer virtually cancel themselves out in conflict but, like a well drilled team, work in increasing unison so that the individual personality brings from within itself a new force which plays into the external pattern of karmic effects. To put it provocatively, the active Self remakes the past from its operational point in the immediate present— something clearly unthinkable if one's mind sees life only from the angle of linear and sequential time. Yet it is not only believed, but known to be so, by the mind which can effectively hold the two views of causality on the one hand and, on the other, what, for lack of a western word, we call Taoism or synchronistic, co-incidental science (the word co-incidental, being hyphenated, designates the meaningful incidence at a given time and place of the various factors involved in any situation).

The co-incidence of outer and inner events and situations can perhaps best be illustrated by reference to the horoscope of a new-born child. For despite what one scholar described as its "intrinsic improbability," astrology, properly used and understood, has proved to many intelligent people—including Dr. C. G. Jung- —that a chart of the heavens at the time of a birth can give endless insight into the child's latent character. And, later in life, because the relation of the stars and planets have changed, it will help to indicate what concatenated "influences" are at work on and in him at any time. This does not mean that the individual is fated from birth to be the slave of his nativity, because, as I have said, the nuclear Self is not a passive onlooker in the development of a character, but plays an increasingly powerful part in the process, as he becomes self-realizing and self-actualizing.

So while it is true that, say, a "badly aspected" Saturn may lead to a frustrated, held-down personality, or Uranus may indicate the likelihood of upheavals and changes, the wise man, by understanding *and accepting* himself in a positive manner, will discover how, by cooperating with the forces in his personality—the gods both within and outside himself—he can change his whole attitude toward life and find harmony and happiness. The Saturn-bound person, when he has performed the magic act of self-acceptance, may find the most obstinate obstacles melt away in a manner which seemed impossible so long as he feared, rejected, or tried to escape from them. The Uranian may find a quiet harmony coming into his life. It is as if the change inside the personality also changes the environment. Or, a physically sick or disabled person may find out how to live happily with his disability, "staying with it" instead of fighting it, and so halving its pain. Victor Frankl, in *Man in Search of Meaning*, points out that the inalienable freedom to *choose one's attitude of mind* persists, even in a Nazi prison camp.

How to bring about this change is an individual matter. But in general terms it comes about as a result of any kind of yoga, including that of psychological analysis of the right kind. The key to it is self-knowledge and self-understanding through deep self-examination.

Happiness is not found by trying to escape suffering but by realizing that it is something one has evoked by one's own acts. So also is pleasure: one should enjoy ("find joy in") the pleasant things of life, and avoid mortification (to mortify means to kill) from the detached central point which is Self in the deeper sense, not the reflections of that Self in the desire-field of personal ego.

Thus it would seem that the "Man of Tao," or Confucian "Superior Man," the true yogi or rishi, mystic or saint, is one who, in whatever terms, or by whatever

method—whether it be meditation or psychological
analysis—brings order into the house of his personality.
He becomes the arbiter of his own acts. He will still,
since he is human, "generate" karma; but not only will
he, step by step, learn how to deal with what lies behind
him in terms of time; he will find the way to resolve, at
the existential instant in which it occurs, any new karma
which he creates. Then the back-log, if any, shrinks
until it disappears altogether and he is free. He "rules
his stars," not by attempting to force his will on the
universe, but by learning its laws and becoming its completely obedient servant. In this way, as against that of
the prekarmic, premental animal, he will now work
from the center of his being as a self-aware, self-understanding individual, the Perfected Man.

* * * * *

To sum up on a practical level, the active, self-
actualizing man needs to realize that:

(a) Karma is geared into the whole cosmic process;

(b) It represents the personal and individual impact
of this process on himself;

(c) It is his selfhood which initiates the chain of cause
and effect which we call karma. This selfhood may be
strong or weak, depending on the degree to which he
has ordered and taken control of the forces within his
personal field. If it is weak, he is carried more or less
passively by the ebb and flow of the collective forces
around him. If it is strong, he, step-by-step, takes
charge of his own destiny.

(d) Selfhood or self-identity is acquired, not by attempts to force matters into the shape one believes one
desires, but by understanding and self-awareness. For
as one not only knows but, as Teilhard puts it, learns to
see oneself in the process of knowing, what has been an
indirect, more or less ineffective impact of the true Self
on the environment becomes more direct and coopera-

tive with the total cosmic process we know as Nature or God.

(e) To do this well requires a mind developed sufficiently to integrate what, in one aspect, is the duality of the ordinary science of causality with that of what Jung has called synchronicity, or *Tao*.

(f) When this occurs, it is as if, from the immediate *now*, the Self as it were remakes the past, insofar as it changes the immediate impact of ancient causes on the present. The resultant is modified by the Self at the moment when that past impinges on it at any instant of time.

(g) This, clearly, from the immediate instant, influences the future: for the wise man, ideally, deals in a positive way with events as they occur and leaves no backlog of unresolved material to be carried forward. There are no new causal residues to bring out effects at a later date, and the individual becomes free in the deeper sense, ready for the great step which is known as entry into *Nirvana, Moksha,* liberation, or salvation.

(h) Such principles, even if only partially understood and practiced, have an immediate practical lesson for us in our daily lives. For they show us that karma is no accident, but that, in its exactness, we are born at a particular time and a particular place because, whether we like it or not, it is the only proper one, and so the best for us at the time. This should make us think very carefully before we try (as so many do today) to uproot ourselves from our own culture and embrace an alien one, seeking to become Hindus or Zenists or Sufis when we are born in the West; or, in reverse, trying to turn into Europeans or Americans when born in the East. The result is rarely a success, because the would-be convert is in effect a fugitive from the life he has "earned" karmically for himself. He has run away from reality into what, psychologically, is fantasy, however genuine the actual religion or creed he adopts. In gen-

eral (though there are a few exceptions among individuals who have not fallen into the trap which awaits
most of these transvestites), the step they have taken in
uprooting themselves from the culture where they belong is backward from, not forward to, Reality. Sooner
or later they will have to discover that spiritual freedom
is to be found at home, not in a foreign land, however
seemingly romantic and "holy" it is supposed to be: to
the one who has the eyes to see, London, Los Angeles,
and Paris are just as spiritual and holy as Varanasi,
Mecca and Jerusalem.

There is another lesson to be learned from karma,
which we would do well to introduce into our way of
thinking, if not yet into our speech. It is becoming
increasingly important today when men and women vie
with one another for sexual equality. It is to be hoped
that at the back of this there lies a profound intuition,
that we are in reality neither men nor women, but
human monads, and as such at once sexless and also
having the qualities of both masculinity and femininity.
But the "Ring-Pass-Not" of the monad is, in each incarnation, sexed as either masculine or feminine; and,
since the incarnation represents the fruits of karmic
experience, there is a reason why the Self is, for awhile,
embodied in a male or female body.

The task of the would-be wise individual is to live with
his/her sex, learning the deeper meaning of masculinity
or femininity while at the same time not diminishing or
reneging on the spiritual and mental qualities of the
other sex, but bringing them into play from within. This
integrates the masculine or the feminine "unconscious"
with the conscious and operative sexuality of the outer
garment of that unconsciousness. This is a fact recognized by the better kind of depth psychologist, notably
by Jung and his colleagues, where the man's "anima" or
the woman's "animus" is taken as an important "archetypal image" in every self-realizing student. A

"man" should live like a man while using his feminine intuitions and feelings; a "woman" should be able to be feminine without either weakening her masculinity or trying to become dominant and "masculine" in the wrong way.

This, of course, is a far cry from saying that we should not study other philosophies and religions. On the contrary, the wider our scope the better, provided we add to our mental knowledge the supraintellectual function of understanding, and thus acquire wisdom. What is harmful to the individual is the emotive quality of thinking that, by becoming outwardly a Hindu swami or Buddhist monk or Japanese Zenist, one is liberating oneself from one's karma. At the same time, we need to discover that the Liberation which the serious and realistic seeker is trying to reach can be found anywhere, anytime, when the student is inwardly ready. It is probably so near that we cannot touch it because we reach too far, so obvious that we cannot see it; and, moreover, it may even be that we have already touched it but, with minds full of doctrines, mental concepts, rites and observances, we cloud over the Vision which our inward eye has given us. Rituals, meditations, disciplines and the like may help, but they do so only for a time. After that they become clogs in the wheel of progress, addictions like that to any other drug. It takes courage to drop all the contents of one's mind, accumulated through aeons of time, and to proceed unfettered into the darkness, relying not even upon a nameless and faceless god, but upon one's own individual Self. Yet, I believe, such is the way in which the individual finds release and mastery over the wheel of rebirth and of karma.

Part Two

There is more to be said about karma than I have written above. For it would seem that the goal of every human being can be summarized by saying that *nirvana,* *moksha,* liberation, salvation can be reached only when that person is karma-free, that is, when there is no backlog of causes playing into his present state; when he is, so to speak, completely gathered up into the immediate *now.* But so long at least as he is incarnate, his very existence, his presence in the manifested universe, means that he is generating karma at every instant and by his every act, physical or psychic. The difference between such a man and the rest is, however, that he has found the means to resolve this karma at the very instant it is generated and as he passes from moment to moment in time.

In principle, this means that he has learned to attune himself absolutely to the cosmic pattern as it is at that moment so that there is no kind of stress or conflict between what is taking place within his individual monadic field and what is happening in the universe as a whole.

Whether we look upon the universe as proceeding through time from past to future, or whether we see it as a constant dynamic state in which creation and destruction (or better, resolution) are always at work together, each fleeting moment can be seen as an integrated whole of which we are a part. Our job, then, is to bring ourselves into step with the universal rhythm and to keep pace with its forward movement. This is the whole purpose behind what we know as religion and *should* be the aim of all religious creeds and disciplines.

In other words, there is a personal and individual impact of karma, in the greater sense of movement in the cosmos, on our own individual monadic field. This field, as I have suggested, centers round its own "sun" or "god," the true Self, and it is because this Self is not yet in command of its field that man finds himself in trouble, out of tune with the world in which he lives. He will suffer for this until harmony is restored, not be-

cause God punishes, but because <u>free will</u> enables him
to act differently from other monads, both on his own
level and at the levels which contain him (e.g., the biosphere of the earth, the solar system and so on). Erich
Fromm has said that the first genuinely human act was
when, in Eden, Adam and Eve disobeyed Nature (God)
and asserted themselves in such a way that they cut
across the laws of prehumanity, thus beginning the long
karmic road.

<u>Man's task is thus to restore himself to a state of
nature, of harmony with the world, to return to God-
—without, however, losing the precious things he has</u>
acquired during his "estrangement." One of these is the
<u>individuality,</u> the sense of Selfhood, which distin-
guishes him from the prehuman animal.

<u>This Selfhood,</u> however, has to become something
<u>very different from the little selfhood of the psycholog-
ical ego,</u> which is constantly obtruding itself and inter-
fering with events in daily life, demanding the fulfil-
ment of instinctive desire.

<u>The process of extracting Self from egoism</u> is the aim
of every true religious school. Moreover, as the student
moves along the paths laid down by these religions, he
has step by step to <u>find his own individual discipline and
proceed alone and unaided except from within himself</u>.

It is here that the modern schools of the <u>deepest of
depth psychology</u> can be of immense use, because
(thanks to Freud, however much we may disagree with
his interpretations) they teach us to <u>confront ourselves,</u>
and suggest the means of "getting at" the unknown side
of ourselves which we call the <u>unconscious</u>. The same
could, in theory, be done by a direct study of the forces,
psychic and physical, named by science but known more
intimately to us as archetypal images of gods, heroes,
symbols. A valuable way to begin on this way is that
adumbrated by Freud in his *Psychpathology of Everyday
Life*—even if we find his preoccupation with the physi-

cal body inadequate and tiresome. For he draws our attention to the meaningfulness of mistakes, slips of the tongue, and the "irrational" world of dreams and fantasies. We find meaning in these things when we learn to study them; and they will start us on the discovery of this inner field around the Self, the unconscious. One needs to go through this stage; it leads on to what are really the grass roots of man's actual quality.

Now we begin to meet with the essential Man, in the form of what Jung has called the archetypal images: the gods of the pantheon within us, figures of power and charismatic value which are capable, as we allow them to operate on and in us, of carrying us from the realm of *the gods* to that of *God*, the numinous Source of all things. We are, in other words, entering the world of myth, that is, of the deeper truths about ourselves and our origins as human entities. Myth has been said by Annie Besant, as well as by C. G. Jung, to be the true history of man both individual and as a species, and to represent his attempts at spiritual self-realization in the form of dramatic stories.

As we learn about myth as applied to each of us individually, we begin to take control over our destinies, i.e., of our relationship to the Cosmic Myth which is the Universe as a whole. This is worth realizing, as it is clearly much closer to our daily experience to think in terms of myth and of gods and goddesses, of symbols and sacramental acts and objects, than to use the languages of physics and mathematics. For while they are equally valid, they are much more remote for the ordinary individual.

Each of us, as a monad, is the expression of a personal and individual myth; it is for each of us to fulfill and complete that myth in terms of the personal, subjective drama we touch in our dreams, visions, inner experiences. For as we work it out, we bring our nuclear Self into its true place as the center of our personal lives.

Also, by ordering the "gods" within us, we catch up, as it were, with the cosmic situation as it moves from moment to moment in constant flow, and so find at once complete freedom, the "liberation" so often spoken of today. But, paradoxically, we do so by becoming completely obedient and at one with the world we call external to our personal monadic selves. This, in another way, is to say that we free ourselves from the law of karma by becoming part of the universal karma which is the very life of a manifested Godhead.

What it amounts to is that we cannot know God without knowing and understanding the gods: those gods which are both cosmic forces and forces within our own monadic sphere. We may know all the teachings about the universe (I use the word "teachings" rather than "fact" because most of the facts about the cosmos are quite beyond our immediate experience, and so have to be taken as unproved hypotheses) but they will have little value or significance to us unless we know our own home-self, our own domestic gods, the actors in the individual myth which is each one of us. The fact that (like the monadic principle outlined earlier in this article) this myth is based on the same blueprint (see comparative mythology and its exegesis in psychological and religious texts) with the same basic figures of hero, villain, demonic forces, redeemer, etc., does not detract from this principle. The pantheon is in us, but it functions in its own individual way, this way being linked with the general pattern exhibited in the universe at any moment of time.

As these gods represent karma in a cosmic sense, so do they represent karma in relation to our own individuality. Liberation and *nirvana* ("the cessation of error and of strife") comes when the individual monadic pattern harmonizes with the cosmic one and so becomes integrated with it. We are then "united with God the Father" and so become the pattern of the universal Christ or Buddha.

SUGGESTED READING

The Stanzas of Dzyan
The major works of H. P. Blavatsky.
The major writings of J. Krishnamurti.
The major works of C. G. Jung.
Experiment in Depth by P. W. Martin (Routledge, London).
Cutting Through Spiritual Materialism by Chögyam Trungpa (Shamballa).
Patterns of Prophecy, Alan Vaughan (Turnstone, London).
Essays by Albert Einstein, Fred Hoyle, and other modern scientists.
The Symbolic and the Real by Ira Progoff
The Psychopathology of Everyday Life; The Interpretation of Dreams by Sigmund Freud (various publishers).

6.

Infinite Continuity In Multimillionfold Diversity

ARTHUR ROBSON

Infinite continuity, but *not* on a level, nor in a dead straight line. We find everywhere this constantly recurring theme of the periodicity of nature, activity alternating with inactivity; broad daylight with its round of activity, followed by night and sleep or comparative inactivity; spring and summer with their growth and activity followed by autumn and winter and cold and a slackening off; birth, youth, and the activities of vigorous manhood or womanhood, and then old age and finally death. There are still larger circles which we discern: the gradual rise of a nation, for example, with a flowering of the arts, literature, commerce etc., followed by its gradual decline and fall. Then we observe that an age of enlightenment, enduring for about a millenium, is followed by a dark age enduring for approximately another millenium. And there are larger circles still, which tell us of warm periods in the life of our planet, alternating with ice ages, when its life was reduced to a minimum.

Why then should we be surprised when we are told that life is a continual ebb and flow, which goes on from one incarnation to another, from life in one body, through death and a period in Devachan ("which may last for years, decades, centuries and milleniums, of ten-times multiplied by something more. It all depends upon the duration of Karma.")[1] to life in another body.

Now, do not make the mistake of confusing this with the idea of transmigration of souls, according to which when one dies one may be born again as a bird or beast. In Shakespeare's *Merchant of Venice* Gratiano says:

> Thou almost mak'st me waver in my faith,
> To hold opinion with Pythagoras,
> That souls of animals infuse themselves
> Into the trunks of men.

Some people see this to be a declaration of the theory of transmigration of souls. But such a theory is against the normal order of things, and Pythagoras never held it. He held, it is true, that "the souls of animals infuse themselves into the trunks of men," but *not the other way about,* which is what the transmigration of souls implies. Once we have attained to life as a human being, we never revert to incarnation as animals.

The common objection to the theory of reincarnation is, "Why don't we remember our past lives?" It's true that ordinarily we cannot recall any part of our past lives, but in everything we do our past is plainly seen. Obvious examples are the natural inclinations of each of us, each characteristically different in its own way, outstanding among them being great musicians, artists, mathematicians, etc., too numerous to catalogue. Some may say, "If I had had the opportunity and devoted myself to it, I could have become as great as X." But is this true? No. The greatness of X has grown by his repeatedly doing through countless lives the things in which he excels. We have to get rid of the notion that such an excellence is a "talent" or "gift." Such "gifts" come from one's having sown well and truly through many lives and, in due course of time, reaping the fruit of that sowing.

There is not a single trait of character, not a mannerism, but has its history—often a history full of events and absorbing interest—the beginnings of which lie so far back in time that the thought of trying to discover them is staggering. It is this mass of habits, mannerisms, and peculiarities of our natures, that which we know as "character," that constitutes our Karma, the record of our entire past, the fount and origin of all the pleasure and pain that we experience. So we get a multimillion-fold diversity, as each person has a character which is individually *his own*. And so it will remain till the end of time, because no one can change his nature, although we go on *evolving from within.* The *Bhagavad Gita* tells us:

> Therefore, without attachment, do Karma that is necessary, for by doing Karma without attachment man obtains supreme bliss. As the ignorant act from attachment to Karma, O Bharata, so should the wise act without attachment, having the common welfare at heart.[2]

The Mahatma K.H. has written:

> Your acts in the past. . . .cannot be obliterated, for they are indeliby stamped upon the record of Karma.[3]

It is this that we take with us from one life to another. Each trait of character is but a little eddy that goes down the years with us, circling in our life long after the original circumstances that called it into being have been left behind and completely forgotten. Dr. Ananda Coomaraswamy, in speaking of "the momentum of antecedent karma," refers to "the brilliant simile of the potter's wheel, which continues to turn after the hand of the potter is removed."

The word "Karma" comes from the Sanskrit term for "doing," and it is used of all that we do habitually. Of course, we must not only take into consideration the Karma of *merit*, but also that of *demerit,* earned by our past misdeeds.

As the doctrines of Reincarnation and Karma have been revived during the last hundred years, largely through the efforts of The Theosophical Society, it would be well to see how that Society came to be founded.

> After nearly a century of fruitless search, our chiefs had to avail themselves of the only opportunity to send out a European *body* upon European soil to serve as a connecting link between that country and our own.[4]

Thus it was that Russian born H.P. Blavatsky, after being instructed by the Mahatmas in a secluded valley in the Himalayas, joined with Henry Steel Olcott in the United States of America in founding The Theosophical Society in New York in 1875. This was a unique opportunity to spread the wisdom of the Sages throughout the world.

H.P. Blavatsky wrote *Isis Unveiled* in 1877, and followed it with *The Secret Doctrine* in 1888; each work contained a wealth of most diversified information. Meanwhile the Mahatmas M. and K.H., who had made contact with the two English gentlemen, A.P. Sinnett and A.O. Hume, and had entered into correspondence with them, were disseminating the same truths through them. Although it was not intended that the letters should be published without having been first edited by a competent authority, they have come to us unedited as *The Mahatma Letters to A.P. Sinnett*, published in 1923, about forty years after they were written.

Let me say straight away that the Mahatmas have no place for the usual idea of God in their philosophy.

> The word "God" was invented to designate the unknown cause of those effects which man has either admired or dreaded without understanding them, and since we claim that we are able to prove what we claim—i.e., the knowledge of that cause and causes—we are in a position to maintain there is no God or Gods behind them.[5]

But this does not mean that there is no room for supernormal beings in occult philosophy.

> We believe in Dhyan Chohans or Planetaries, and endow them with a universal mind.[6]

But they all form part of the One Life and there is nothing outside it, which an extraterrestrial God would have to be. Even the highest Planetaries were, at some time in the remote past, mortal men such as we; and although they are now supernormal, they passed millions of millions of years ago through the same round of evolutionary growth as we are undergoing today.

Dhyan Chohan (pronounced "Jän Chohan," the "J" being given the same phonetic value as in English words) means "Lord of Wisdom," and corresponds vaguely to the Angels of Christian belief. Planetaries are higher still, and may be said to correspond to Archangels.

It is so very difficult to give an idea of what we are trying to describe except by quoting the Master K.H. who says:

> We will perhaps be near correct to call it *infinite life* and the source of all life, visible and invisible, an essence inexhaustible, ever present, in short Swabhavat. (Swabhavat in its universal application, Fohat when manifesting throughout our phenomenal world, or rather the visible universe, hence in its limitations.)[7]

"Swabhavat" is Sanskrit for "self-existent." "Fohat" is a Turanian word which seems to have been derived from "Swabhavat," the initial, unstressed syllable (*swa*) having been elided, and the rest (*bhavat*) having been corrupted to suit linguistic demands, and limited in its application to our visible universe. So Swabhavat is the *infinite life* of which we form part. H.P.Blavatsky says:

> Throughout the first two parts it has been shown that, at the first flutter of renascent life Swabhavat passes, at every new rebirth of Kosmos, from an inactive state into one of intense activity; that it differentiates, and then begins its work through differentiation. This work is KARMA.[8]

This means that Swabhavat goes through much the same process as before the old Kosmos passed out of existence; it is, remember, the same infinite life, and the birth of a new Kosmos is much the same as the birth of a new day, or the birth of a new life, when one returns to one's usual activities. The only God in all this is the "God within my breast." This truth is so stupendous that we find it hard to take it in. Yet there was one who, with Olympian wisdom, perceived it for herself and, furthermore, in Orphean tones proclaimed it for all to hear, even at the risk of being considered shockingly presumptuous and sacrilegious.

IMMORTALITY

No coward soul is mine,
    No trembler on the world's storm-troubled sphere;
I see Heaven's glories shine
    And faith shines equal, arming me from fear.
O God within my breast,
    Almighty, ever-present Deity!
Life—that in me has rest,
    As I—undying Life—have power in thee!
Vain are the thousand creeds
    That move men's heart; unutterably vain:
Worthless as withered weeds,
    Or idlest froth amid the boundless main,
To waken doubt in one
    Holding so fast by Thy infinity;
So surely anchored on
    The steadfast rock of immortality.
With wide-embracing love
    Thy spirit animates eternal years,
Pervades and broods above,
    Changes, sustains, dissolves, creates and rears.
Though earth and man were gone,
    And suns and universes ceased to be,
And Thou wert left alone,
    Every Existence would exist in Thee.
There is not room for Death,
    Nor atom that his might could render void;
Thou—THOU art Being and breath,

And what THOU art may never be destroyed.
                                    Emily Bronte.*

Set your heart at rest. The sky is the limit, if I may borrow a cliché from television. You may go on evolving until eternity. In fact you *have* to go on evolving, and chiefly *by your own efforts*. The Mahatma M. has written:

> The task is difficult and K. H., in remembrance of old times, when he loved to quote poetry, asks me to close my letter with the following to your address
> Does the road wind up-hill all the way?
> Yes, to the very end.
> Will the day's journey take the whole long day?
> From morn to night, my friend.
>
> Knowledge for the mind, like food for the body, is intended to feed and help growth, but it requires to be well digested, and the more thoroughly and slowly the process is carried out, the better both for the body and the mind.[9]

There is no easy road to Adeptship. The Mahatma K. H. has written:

> The fact is that to the last and supreme initiation every chela (and even some adepts) is left to his own device and counsel. We have to fight our own battles, and the familiar adage—"the adept *becomes,* he is not *made*"—is true to the letter. Since every one of us is the *creator* and producer of the cause that leads to such or some other results, we have to reap but what we have sown.[10]

According to this, it may seem that Adepts are rather callous, leaving chelas (and also some Adepts, who insist on working things out for themselves) to their own devices. On the contrary, they are filled with a most intense compassion, and do what is best for us. What would you do if you noticed an unhatched chicken trying to peck its way out of its egg? To remove the

*This splendid poem has been set to music in *Six Songs to Poems of Emily Bronte* by John Joubert, obtainable from Novello & Co., Borough Green, Sevenoaks, Kent TW 15 8DT, England.

eggshell would result in premature exposure and the chicken would be so much the weaker. No, let it peck its own way out of the shell, as the mother hen lets it do, while she clucks encouragement. The same applies to a man trying to break his way into Adeptship. The sincere aspirant would very much prefer to be left to work his way unassisted.

To understand this let us follow the course of evolution. Until the animal stage one has been entirely under the influence of Brahma. Now Brahma is not a god, nor is it a person, nor any other being. Brahma is only an idea, the expansive force of nature. The Mahatma M. has defined the word:

> Brahma, from the root "brih," the Sanskrit for "to expand, grow or fructify," Brahma being but the vivifying *expansive* force of nature in its eternal evolution.[11]

In all animals we find the natural impulse to expand. In the human being this remains for a long time the dominant urge. We find him increasing his wealth, his influence, his power, his knowledge, his skill. But at the same time he learns to be of increasing service to others in many ways. After all, social life becomes ever more interdependent. A new force has become apparent, that of Vishnu, from the Sanskrit *vish,* meaning "to serve." Vishnu is not a god, any more than is Brahma. At first it is inseparable from Brahma. People do service only because *it pays them.* Coal owners and miners, electric boards and electricians, railway boards and railwaymen, etc., all insist on getting as much as they can out of their activities. The countries that produce oil, sugar, etc., hold out for the highest prices obtainable. There is little "service" about it, and the scramble for more and more of what each can get leads to further and further inflation, sending up the prices higher and higher. There is only one way to stop all this, and that is by people of real good will with a true sense of *service* declining to take more than they really need.

Well, suppose that we were truly *social* and the spirit of service came into its own! Then we should have a true reign of Vishnu, everybody doing all they could to assist wherever they could—the teacher, merchant, manufacturer, judge, etc., all giving of their best. Would everybody be forever happy? Apparently not. Certainly not for very long. Many would prefer to do things for themselves. Now a new force would be required in the Guru, that of detachment, Shiva, a force which allows him to stand aside and allow others to work things out for themselves. We all tend, after having reached a particular stage in our evolution, to identify ourselves with Shiva. The Adept lives in this state almost continuously.

> The adept sees and feels and lives in the very source of all fundamental truths—the Universal Spiritual Essence of Nature, Shiva, the Creator, the Destroyer and the Regenerator. As Spiritualists of today have degraded "Spirit," so have the Hindus degraded Nature by their anthropomorphistic conceptions of it.[12]

The editors of the third edition of the *Letters* have altered the word, "anthropomorphistic" to "anthropomorphic." But in so doing they have missed the whole point of the Mahatma's having to coin a word to convey his meaning. A figure with four faces or four arms is certainly *not* in human form, and can only be said to be in "humanized" form.

Shiva is said to be the Destroyer, but the *Destroyer of Karma*. Shiva is the embodiment of *sacrifice*, and in sacrifice one approaches the divine.

It may be thought that when an Adept attains Nirvana he turns his back on life as something with which he has finished and which no longer concerns him. But, paradoxical as it may seem, he is enabled to withdraw completely from life only because of his having completely merged himself in, and attained perfect At-one-ment, with life. The Mahatma K. H. has written:

Oh, for the final Rest! For that Nirvana where—"to be one with Life, yet—to live not."[13] [But this] State of absolute Rest in which all things objective are forgotten[14]

does not last forever. In due course the Nirvanee returns to consciousness of objective life as a Dhyan Chohan.

Although the Dhyan Chohans have attained complete detachment from life, they do not remain spectators of it. The Mahatma speaks of them as "the protectors of our Race and the Trustees for those that are coming."[15]

Elsewhere the Mahatma, speaking of the animal and vegetable kingdoms, says:

As we have our Dhyan Chohans so have they in their several kingdoms elemental guardians and are well taken care of in the mass as is humanity in the mass.[16]

The Dhyan Chohans take care, not only of the living humanity, but also of the disembodied egos.

Every such "world" within the Sphere of Effects has a Tathagata, or "Dhyan Chohan" to protect and watch over, not to interfere with it.[17]

They protect the victims of accident and murder.

The Dhyan Chohans who have no hand in the guidance of the *living* human Ego, protect the helpless victim when it is violently thrust out of its element into a new one, before it is matured and made fit and ready for it.[18]

They guide the birth-seeking ego to the place of its rebirth:

And it is that variety which guides the temporary personal *Ego* into the current which will lead him to be reborn in a lower or higher condition in the next world of causes. Everything is so harmoniously adjusted in nature—especially in the subjective world—that no mistake can ever be committed by the Tathagatas—or Dhyan Chohans—who guide the impulses.[19]

They not only watch life which is already in being, but also give the impulse which goes to the making of new systems of life.

At the beginning of the solar manwantara the hitherto subjective elements of the material world now scattered in cosmic dust—receiving their impulse from the new Dhyan Chohans of the solar system (the highest of the old ones having gone higher)—will form into primordial ripples of life, and separating into differentiating centres of activity combine in a graduated scale of seven stages of evolution.[20]

They do not *create* a new solar system, any more than a gardener creates a plant when he sows a seed, and so initiates the life cycle of a plant. The cosmic atom is *in itself* potentially a Dhyan Chohan, just as much as the seed is potentially a plant and, just as the gardener creates conditions which are favorable to the potentiality in the seed developing into reality, so do the Dhyan Chohans create conditions which allow of the cosmic atoms starting on the long road of evolution which leads up to the Dhyan Chohan, or Planetary Spirit.

The potentiality which develops finally in a perfected planetary spirit lurks in, *is* in fact that primordial cosmic atom.[21]

It is this potentiality that gradually unfolds itself *from within*—"evolutes"—and, having attained humanhood, goes on evoluting until it appears as a perfect Planetary Spirit.

Evoluting from cosmic matter—which is *akasa,* the primeval not the secondary plastic medium, or Ether of Science instinctively suspected, unproven as the rest—man first evolutes from this *matter* in its most sublimated state, appearing at the threshold of Eternity as a perfectly *Etherial*—not Spiritual Entity, say—a Planetary Spirit.[22]

A Dhyan Chohan seems to us an absolutely perfect being. But there are degrees of perfection even among them. This is very hard for us to conceive, but the following would probably be an analogy.

We may describe any person as a tightrope walker when he has attained sufficient skill to be able to walk the rope without falling off. This corresponds to Nirvana. But there are refinements in the tightrope walker's art which he will go on acquiring. Similarly, a Dhyan Chohan, having attained Nirvana, acquires immunity from falling back into the round of birth and death. But there are refinements of spirituality which he goes on acquiring after that. Having already learnt to dispense with a physical body, he learns to dispense with one after another of the superphysical bodies, and so becomes in time formless, an "*A*rupa-deva" or formless Dhyan Chohan, the whole process taking a manvantara. What becomes of the Dhyan Chohan, after they become formless is a mystery even to the Adepts.

As to the winner of that race throughout the worlds——the Spiritual Ego, he will ascend from star to star, from one world to another, circling onward to rebecome the once pure Planetary Spirit, then higher still, to finally reach its first starting point, then—to merge into MYSTERY. No adept has ever penetrated beyond the veil of primitive Kosmic matter. The highest, the most perfect vision is limited to the universe of *Form* and *Matter*.[23]

References

1. *The Mahatma Letters to A.P. Sinnett*, transcribed and compiled by A.T. Barker, 3rd ed., Adyar: Theosophical Publishing House, 1962, p. 103.
2. *The Bhagavad Gita*, III: 19, 25.
3. Letters from the Masters of the Wisdom, 2nd Series, p. 61.
4. Barker, op.cit., p. 201.
5. Ibid., p. 52
6. Ibid., p. 55.
7. Ibid., p. 89
8. *The Secret Doctrine*, 3rd ed., I:695.
9. Barker, op.cit., p. 258
10. Ibid., p. 305.
11. Ibid., p. 71.
12. Ibid., p. 241.
13. Ibid., p. 113.

14. Ibid., p. 195.
15. Ibid., p. 154.
16. Ibid., p. 95.
17. Ibid., p. 105.
18. Ibid., p. 128.
19. Ibid., p. 100.
20. Ibid., p. 96.
21. Ibid., p. 88.
22. Ibid., p. 45.
23. Ibid., p. 47.

7.

In This Silence, Sanity Is Born
Karma as the Order of the Universe

GEORGE KOCH

It may seem unsophisticated to say so, but it is important to realize at the outset what great privilege and opportunity is ours in being able to consciously study the mystery of Karma, for most of us live most of our lives ignorant of both its existence and its workings. Having now awakened to it, however recently, we have before us the possiblity of a fundamental transformation in the quality and nature of our lives. Here, in this mystery, lies the final sense and order of the universe, presenting itself in all forms, gross and subtle. Here, through this mystery, we may understand profoundly what it is to be one with life, to live in and with its order, to conduct our individual lives integrally in harmony with the one life manifesting through us.

Though the substance of Karma is a simple truth, its attainment may be a difficult and frustrating process, for the deeper we penetrate its mystery, the more unlike our preconceptions it becomes. Karma is but a word used to refer to a cosmic process, finally to the cosmic process that orders all things. It will without effort bear up under the closest and most penetrating inquiry, revealing to anyone sheath upon sheath of ever more subtle mystery, of ever more simple truth. The more penetrating the inquiry, the more unlike the initial understandings will the truth be. It is thus crucial that we not be led astray by our early openings into this mystery.

When we are first introduced to this great process it is

likely that our perception will show it to be the law of action and reaction in human affairs. "As a man sows, so shall he reap" is the phrase which essentially embodies this view of Karma, and though this is a great truth in itself, deeper aspects remain yet to be uncovered. Karma, the superconscious process that teaches to man and woman the meaning of just and true action, is beyond this also the teacher of all mysteries. Karma, ultimately, is not merely a moral equalizer, but rather the very order of the universe itself; it moves within the spheres of justice and morality, but is not limited to them.

The contradictions that we come upon between our early understandings, profound and moving though they may have been at their time, and our later and more radical discoveries, are necessarily illusory. As the bud and the flower are vastly different, and yet quite the same, so are our early and later understandings of Karma seemingly in contradiction, yet truly harmonious.

If we seem then to wander into areas unfamiliar and without markings, let us be aware that what we witness cannot be confined by our early understandings, for it is behind and beyond all, is THAT from which all things spring. This is the great teacher, Karma, for being all things, it teaches all things, giving to each only what each is prepared to receive, without favor or dislike.

All morality, save the highest, is principled. To the most insecure, and therefore the most violent, the principle is simple and unwavering: survival at any cost. As education and civilization grow in a society, this one principle is modified, taking on nuances and exceptions. It widens into many areas of social intercourse, dictates dress and eating habits, governs what violence is acceptable and what is not. Men and women begin to become aware of the existence of principle, and morality and social justice take birth. Still, at the base of all this, hidden deep among the many philosophies, and simmering among the most noble of ideals and causes, the one principle continues to exist: survival. All social moralities, without exception, are modifications of this one base, and to a greater or lesser extent make it visible in their laws and social codes.

While it is important to see clearly the absolute rulership of this principle in all social morality, it would be a grave error to dismiss all such moralities as useless attempts at order and no more, for they surely are the first recognition of Karma by humanity, and though the perception is dim, yet itis there.

The early evolutionary consciousness, in its naturally confused and insecure awakening, has given rise to violence and social chaos; all about, nature demonstrates to this dim perception the vastness of its order: it shows in the regularity of its seasons, in the passing of day and night, in the cycles of the body and all living things, in the absolute fulfillment of its laws that order exists. Within the chaos of human activity man tries to construct a parallel order, and with it to find a security, a protection from the chaos his unconsciousness has brought. Yet the imitation of order is not the same as order itself, and though man brings refinement upon refinement to his imitation, it is still made in chaos, and chaos it must contain. Not until the unconscious itself gives way can true order prevail. Through the imitation of order the one principle, survival, continues in all modifications.

Finally, the awareness dawns that at the same time as we attempt justice and morality through our laws and social codes, there is another justice at work, far beyond the artificial one that has been created, and quite real and uncompromising in its workings. The order man had dimly perceived around him is there within him as well, independent of any principle he might have constructed, and quite unconcerned with survival.

This order, which we call Karma, exists fully without principle, for principle, the movement for survival and its refinements, is but an artificial standard to which actions are self-consciously compared. Karma, being the order, the causeless, uncreated Principle and law itself, functions without reference or comparison, works as it does without imitation.

This is not a denial of the function of moral principle, for it has its rightful time in the scheme of things, but it is a recognition that the vast motion and order which lie behind and transcend us are not bound by our ideas and responses to them. In a wider sense of course, we too are this vast motion and order, and the chaos we speak of but a passing phantom, yet it is neither wise nor appropriate to confuse these different levels of understanding. Though we may give intellectual or emotional assent to the idea that all is in order, we must likewise know that what is truly order to one perception is just as truly chaos to another. It is only by understanding the chaos we see about us, and not by philosophically denying its existence, that we will finally reach the awareness of the wider truth that knows this chaos as order. Knowing all is in order and believing it are two quite different activities.

Already we have passed through four quite distinct perceptions of Karma: first, the confused and totally self-protective consciousness unaware of anything but threat; second, the beginning though dim perception of an order in the universe outside ourselves; third, the construction of an artificial order in an attempt to control the danger imposed by others equally insecure; and fourth, the recognition that independent of our artificial order there is another, vaster order, both beyond and including our activities, an order which functions free of principle, and by this freedom embodies the highest morality.

The implicit suggestion is that one can live without

principle. It is at first blush a dangerous notion, for were it to be accepted without understanding, it could lead to great violence and social chaos, each doing what he or she pleased with little or no concern for the other. Yet, realistically, this is the state of affairs in which our world presently finds itself. It is not because our actions are without principle that we are violent, but because our principles are born from our insecurity. Whether the principle is the basic one of survival, or a refinement of this in the form of religious dogma, political belief or social custom and law, the basically artificial nature of principled morality always and unavoidably ends in conflict and violence.

The discovery of fundamentally just and true action is not through any emotional or intellectual decision, not through any external or internal command or conceptualization, but rather only through a complete and free opening to the pure order which is in life itself; true morality is not an escape from life, not its imitation. It is life fulfilled, spontaneous, free to act as life requires, and not as dictated by idea or fear.

Having begun to realize the curious sensibility of this unprincipled morality, we come upon an inversion taking place in our lives. Our responsibility is no longer to live up to any principles, however noble, but rather solely to discover the law, the order and truth which are the highest morality. By committing ourselves to any theory or principle, we bind ourselves to our present ignorance, to our present disorder and artificiality.

The state of morality which is beyond principle is psychologically, spiritually free of time, and therefore a time-bound process cannot lead to it. Yet there is value in the time-bound process of living up to principles so long as one has not penetrated their artificial nature. Once this has been done, once it has been seen that principle is not order but an imitation of it, then to bind oneself so becomes a recessive, contrary action.

The existence of ungoverned morality has been
known throughout time; it is spoken of in many ways by
all of the esoteric mystical traditions, though references
to it are often vague and superficially contradictory,
even absurd. Yet this process is evident in many far
quarters of the spiritual community, though it still as
always remains rare. The movement through principles
to an existence utterly free of them is "the gradual path
to sudden awakening." One nurtures in oneself an in-
tensification of principle and morality, a raptured attention to the problem of personal and world violence, a
consequent deep devotion to one spiritual system or
another as a means to resolve this violence. And then,
opening like the first flower among many buds still
closed and protected, one goes beyond the form of
one's own spiritual quest, beyond teacher and religion,
beyond obedience to principle and dictate; one becomes integrally free, integrally loving, moral and incapable of violence, quite unconcerned with survival.
This is the marriage of mind and heart, itself rarely
spoken of in the traditions, itself known as rarely as the
individuals who manifest it.

This marriage is not a co-joining of the intellect and
emotions, for these are to the true mind and heart what
principled morality is to true morality; these are but
shadows of the real existence, servants to it.

When attention is not present, but lost and drifting in
the many fantasies of separative existence, relationships
move quickly to misunderstanding and violence; here
the emotions are called forth—anger or unhappiness
follows. But these emotions are not things to be denied
or controlled, for they are calling us to attention, calling
us away from our heedless and unconscious drifting.
When it is recognized that this is the true and natural
function of emotion, then fear of and entrapment
within it pass away naturally. With attention the need
for this function is past. The cycles of elevation and

depression end, and the true joy of existence is given room to manifest.

So too with the intellect, for while it is not capable of divining absolute truth, it may inquire sufficiently into the relative world to recognize the contradictions of relationship through principle. The intellect can penetrate to frustration, to the veil of vanity, but not beyond.

It is here, at the frustration of the intellect, with the attention called by the emotion, that the final failing of purely separative existence comes before the waiting consciousness. This consciousness, knowing fully and finally that it is both moral and stupid, incapable of living morally in its present state, becomes humble and silent. In this silence, sanity is born. What were once two separate activities, emotion and intellect, what once acted as sentiment and the acquisition of knowledge, now drop away, and but one existence remains. Here it is seen that no marriage has occurred, that the heart has not joined the mind, that no union has taken place because none was required; there is no separation. The mind and heart are one activity, often seen as two by virtue of the manifestation, but finally, beneath it all, one and only one, returned, fulfilled, the same one who began the perilous and unmarked journey, beyond ideas and ideals, unrestricted by principle and vow, ungoverned save by the very order which it is.

8.

Karma in Motion

FELIX LAYTON

Isaac Newton's Third Law of Motion states: "To every action there is
an equal and opposite reaction." This is sometimes thought to be a
statement of the Law of Karma. But Newton's three laws of motion
consider only *physical* force, matter, and motion. Karma includes
life, consciousness, and motive as well as physical force and matter.
This article considers analogies between the limited laws of motion
in the physical world and the all-inclusive principle of karma. It
seeks by considering the laws of physical motion to gain increased
understanding of the universal principle.

Imagine a large, heavy, steel ball at rest on a perfectly
level plane. Imagine further that there is no friction
between the ball and the plane. The ball will remain at
rest until some force makes it move, but if it has once
started to move it will continue to move indefinitely
until something stops it. So said Sir Isaac Newton in his
first Law of Motion, sometimes called the Law of Inertia, a law which has been verified countless times and
seems to be common sense.

Now let a man somehow exert a force on this ball to
push it in a certain direction. Let him continue to push
the ball in the same direction for a long time. As long as
he keeps pushing, the ball will move faster and faster.
How fast it will finally move depends on how hard and
how long the man pushes. This is according to Newton's
second Law of Motion. Since this system is frictionless,
when the man stops pushing, the ball continues to move
in that direction.

Now suppose that the man who worked and pushed
so hard, finds that he made a mistake and pushed the
wrong way, and really wants the ball to go in the oppo-

site direction! The ball now has "within it" the momentum which it stored when the man first pushed, and this
momentum carries it steadily on in the direction of that
first pushing in exact proportion to how hard and how
long the man pushed—and if he pushed hard and long
he will have to push exactly that amount in the opposite
direction before he can stop the ball.

It all works out with absolute exactness. Knowledge
of these laws is the basis for the calculations of forces to
send space capsules on their way. Knowledge of the
same laws enables men to calculate exactly what length
of burn, generating a certain force, will slow, accelerate,
or change direction a certain amount. One astronaut in
flight remarked that we owe it all to Isaac Newton.

The laws seem to be absolute, and they apply not only
to a single object and force but to any system of many
masses and forces. Although first stated by Sir Isaac
Newton they have been realities from the beginning of
creation. They are part of the nature of things—or at
least of the nature of force and matter.

Many people believe that there are correspondences
between physical and spiritual laws. Let us first consider
correspondences between these first two laws and wider
fields.

The law of karma is often compared to Newton's
third Law: "To every action there is an equal and opposite reaction," but perhaps even more interesting correspondences exist with the first two laws, and often
those who quote the third law as an illustration of karma
misunderstand Newton's meaning.

In laboratory experiments, and in the steel ball illustration two factors are involved: *force,* in the example,
applied by the man pushing, and *matter,* in this case a
steel ball. Let these two correspond to life and form or
spirit and matter, or, in our illustration, to the unit of
life or consciousness called a man linked to his bodies or
personality represented by the steel ball. Let us assume

that this life or consciousness functions *within* the body, or the steel ball, and not externally in the same way that the engine functions inside a car.

When such a unit of life, or consciousness, is starting its series of incarnations, it is attached to a body which as yet is at rest, like the ball, for no force has yet acted through it. The boundless level plane on which the ball can be pushed in any direction corresponds to nature, which will allow man to move in any direction he wants—if he works hard enough. As astronaut Eugene Cernan said, "Things may come with difficulty but nothing is impossible to man."

The unit of life, the man, looking out through the senses of the body, sees things he desires. This causes him to work, to strive to obtain them—to move toward them. Suppose he is attracted to wealth. He wants it. He works for it. He struggles and pushes toward it. Perhaps he does this for many lives. In doing so he is building an ever greater momentum in the direction of wealth, for nature gives to man that for which he works. When he obtains it however, he may find that it does not give him the happiness for which he had hoped. He ceases to push and strive toward the goal of wealth. He may continue to coast effortlessly, carried along by his past efforts, but his desires will soon be attracted to another goal and he will begin to try to move in a new direction. However, all his past effort over a long time has built a momentum in the direction of wealth and this keeps him moving in that direction until, after long struggle and pushing against circumstances which seem to frustrate his every effort to move in the new direction, he eventually stops the movement and is free to move in another direction. If this analogy holds, these forces are not merely equal to, they actually are the forces he himself has generated and is now opposing. The more strongly he struggles to stop the ball and move toward the new goal, the more violent will be his conflict with these forces of the past, but the sooner they will be overcome. A believer in karma would say that he is working out his karma.

The shifting of the individual's goal in life usually is toward a nobler goal and comes after some sort of "revelation" or expansion of consciousness. In the nature of things it is then that he tries to move in a new direction and meets the forces he generated earlier, which might be called his karma. Perhaps in this lies an explanation of the phrase, "Whom the Lord loveth he chasteneth." Men consider one whom the Lord loveth to be one who has seen a great goal, such as the service of mankind, and is struggling toward that. He is therefore probably facing momentum and forces he created when moving in other directions and struggling toward less noble goals. The struggle to overcome this momentum would be the chastening.

When an individual performs a "wrong" act, which causes pain to another, he does it only because he knows no better. It is not wrong for him. He is ignorant, as yet. If the karmic consequence of pain returned to him immediately he would probably resent it, fight against it, consider the world unfair to him. He would learn nothing and would probably make the same mistake again. If however, the Lords of Karma defer payment, so to speak, until he "changes direction" and then allow him to meet the consequences of his act, he may then be in a condition of mind which will enable him to learn from the experience of pain and replace the ignorance, which made him perform the wrong act, with wisdom which will prevent him from making that mistake again.

When a cannonball is shot from a cannon, the explosion causes a force to act on the ball and shoot it from the cannon's mouth. If this is the action, then the reaction of which Newton spoke is the force which pushes back on the cannon and causes it to recoil. His third law, applied to this case would mean that the force acting on

the cannonball is equal to the force reacting on the
cannon, and that they act in exactly opposite directions.
This has an interesting correspondence, for just as the
action of firing the shot cannot be performed without
reaction on the cannon, so an individual in this world
cannot perform an action which does not react on
others. He must create karma with one or many others,
or with the whole world, on whom his action produces
an equal and opposite reaction. As with the gun, someone has to absorb the recoil. A man's acts may be of hate,
of love, or mixtures of the two, but whatever they are
they act and react, and these actions and reactions are
always equal and opposite.

In this example the action which shoots the ball in one
direction makes the gun recoil and this reaction or
recoil is absorbed into the great mass of the earth,
disturbing the whole earth's motion and equilibrium.
The shock wave of big guns being fired can be felt to
shake the ground at considerable distances, as the earth
patiently absorbs the shocks. When the action has been
performed, the earth's motion has been altered; it may
have been accelerated, reduced, or pushed sideways.
This alteration to the earth will be too small to measure
but the motion of the ball may be very fast. Eventually
the ball will hit the earth again and stop. When this
happens it returns its energy to the earth; equilibrium is
restored, for it exactly neutralizes the disturbance to the
earth's motion, made when the gun was fired. The ball
may be in the air for a relatively long or short time
before it hits the ground, but eventually the disturbance
to the earth's motion will be neutralized.

There are correspondences between this example
and the law of karma which perhaps emphasize the
realiity of brotherhood for, whether we like it or not,
everyone in the world is affected by every individual
action as the whole world is affected by the firing of
every gun. Let the firing of the cannon in the example

correspond to an act performed by an individual. This greatly affects him as the explosion greatly affects the cannon ball, and it slightly affects the whole world. The condition of imbalance exists between the individual and the world until the karmic consequences are met as the ball hits the earth and equilibrium is restored.

The timing of the reaction is of crucial importance. When does this karmic reaction which restores equilibrium occur? There are references which suggest that at great sacrifice to those who perform the work, karmic consequences may be held back. The moment of impact of the cannon ball, which could be devastating to the individual, may be delayed until the individual is strong enough and in a condition to profit by facing such shocks. One such reference in *Light on the Path* says:

> . . .try to lift a little of the heavy karma of the world; give your aid to the few strong hands that hold back the powers of darkness from obtaining complete victory.[1]

It may well be that in the early stages of man's evolution, and probably today also, men are creating more karma of a destructive, painful type than of a constructive, helpful type. Perhaps in some way, at the cost of untold sacrifice, great Intelligences, Lords of Karma, take some of these ugly, painful forces and store them in their own consciousnesses until humanity and its individuals are ready and able to face them. When that time comes, their sacrifice will be over and the world, which could be overwhelmed if karmic settlements were promptly and automatically made, will literally have been saved. Perhaps such are the Lords of Karma and this is part of their function.

A later reference in *Light on the Path* describes a time when the individual reaches a stage where he can force the karmic consequences of his earlier selfish acts and take back the load which the Lords of Karma have been carrying for him. It suggests that there will now come a great clearing up and an opportunity for learning from this karma of the past as he does his part "to lift a little of the heavy karma of the world." Henceforth he will not be shielded but must face the full karmic consequences of his acts. The passage is an interesting reversal of the way the law of karma is usually stated:

> Out of the silence that is peace a resonant voice shall arise. And this voice will say: It is not well: thou hast reaped, now thou must sow. And knowing this voice to be the silence itself thou wilt obey.[2]

And what about karma-less-ness? It is said that when an individual completes his human pilgrimage he is no longer the slave of karma; he reaches a state of karma-less-ness. This happens, it is said, when his actions are completely selfless and his will (sublimated desires) is one with the One Will. Ordinary actions are self-centered and may be compared to the cannon ball flying within the earth's gravitational field. It is the self-centeredness which eventually draws the reaction back to the doer just as it is the earth's gravitational field which eventually draws the cannon ball back to earth. The completely unselfish action of the Adept, however, is not drawn back and neutralized. It might correspond to shooting a capsule into space which does not return and neutralize itself in earth impact. The laws, possibilities, and limitations of such selfless acts may correspond to completely different phenomena as the weightless world of space travel is completely different from our gravity-bound life on earth.

This article has considered only some details of karma. It has made no attempt to cover the whole sweep of the great law. The examples have been extremely simplified in order to make principles stand out. Only closed systems with two or three factors have been considered. Such simplification is used in early experiments in laboratories where students are learning to understand basic laws. The problems of engineering and physics, which they will study later, involve using these laws in complex open systems with many bodies, forces, actions and reactions, all interacting on one another. The painstaking application of the simple law to one part after another of the complex gives him the capacity to understand, balance, and control the resultants of such interconnected factors. Similarly, there may be principles considered in this article which can be used first to understand, and then to partially control the enormously complicated interacting systems of life which surround us with countless individuals, forces, actions, and reactions. Perhaps this article may suggest further correspondences. It seems a fruitful field. The correspondences have not been suggested as mere intellectual games but as ideas with practical yet spiritual significance.

References

1. Collins, Mabel, *Light on the Path*, Part I, Note to Rule 20.
2. Ibid., Part II, opening lines.

9.

The Meaning of Karma in Integral Philosophy

HARIDAS CHAUDHURI

Volumes have been written on the Law of Karma and its manifold ethico-religious implications aswell as practical bearings upon human life and self-development. The purpose of this paper is to provide a brief account of the ultimate philosophical significance of the Law of Karma, especially in the light of Integralism;[1] the latest development in the Hindu-Buddhist tradition of India.

The fundamental concepts and principles of Integralism have been developed by the author from the teachings of Sri Aurobindo with necessary modifications suggested by the discoveries of modern science and psychology. In respect of its ontological root, it will be shown how the Law of Karma is a logical sequel to the integral world-view or comprehensive awareness of Being.

The major premise of integral philosophy may be spelled out in the form of the following ontological equation:

Being = Cosmic Energy = Entrophy-
Negentropy-Balance
Brahman = Mahāshakti = Tamas-Rajas-Sattva

The meaning of the above equation is that Being (ultimate reality or Brahman) is perfectly identical with, or rather non-different from (advaita), cosmic energy (Mahāshakti), which is the fundamental energy of the cosmic whole.[2] The sign of equation is in this instance the mathematical symbol of the philosophical concept of nonduality. Nonduality means that we are dealing here not with two separate realities, but witt one and the same reality endowed with two inseparable aspects and functions.

Cosmic energy is the basic energy of the cosmic whole from which endless diversities of empirical existence spring into being, in which they all abide, and into which they are dissolved again. The categories of our ordinary thought such as substance, antecedent linear cause, unity, plurality, etc., are inapplicable to the cosmic whole or fundamental energy. Such categories are developed in the human mind as practically useful tools of self-adjustment to the ever-changing environment. In consequence, their scope of application is strictly limited to finite empirical existents or observable phenomena, such as oceans and mountains, rivers and trees, animals and men, stars and galaxies. In so far then as cosmic energy itself is beyond the conceptual tools of intellect, it is incapable of further verbalization (nirguna, anirvachaniya). In respect of its essential being, it is the same as indefinable Being (nirguna Brahman).

Being is the eternally self-existent and self-sufficient ground of the entire universe and its bewildering varieties of existence (nāmarūpa). In so far as it is beyond the scope of application of such ordinary categories of human consciousness as space, time, unchanging substance, antecedent cause, etc. it is logically indeterminable (nirguna, nirākāra). But so far as it is the creative source of the cosmic manifold, it is entirely nondifferent from cosmic energy. It is presumptuous on the part of the human mind to fathom the mystery of Being-Energy (Brahman-Shakti) by thoughtless application of such perceptual categories as space, time, substance, cause, etc.; or such metaphysical categories as matter and mind, nature and spirit; or such theological categories as body and soul, world and God, God and Satan; or such ethical categories as right and wrong, good and evil.

The Triune Structure of Cosmic Energy

The variegated universe in its primordial essence is then cosmic energy. Energy is the harmonious and dynamic unity of three inseparably interrelated forces. The dynamic interactions of these three interrelated modalities of energy give rise to all the fundamental laws of the universe governing our life and destiny. These forces are:

Material force	inertia	entropy	tamas	body
Vital force	activity	negentropy	rajas	life
Mental force	balance	syntropy	sattva	mind

The material force or physical energy is outward self-expression, space-time expansion, extroversion or gradual dissipation of energy. Traceable to this material aspect of energy is the recently discovered scientific truth that the universe in which we live is an expanding universe. Galaxies are tearing away from one another with tremendous speed, as it were, seized with some kind of cosmic hate or repulsion. In the process they are all losing energy little by little, slowly dissipating their life substance in an irretrievable manner. This is known in modern science as the Law of Entropy, the second law of thermodynamics.[3] The law applies not only to intergalactic relations, but to our human relations, too. The more we live an extroverted pattern of living, the more we dissipate our vital energies. The more we engage in the life style of fierce competition and hateful exclusion of one another, the more we squander our spiritual potential and tread the path of perdition. Herein we find the first important implication—the implication on the material level—of the Law of Karma. It is the ethical correlate, in the sphere of human relations, of the scientific Law of Entropy. As we live and act, so we enjoy or suffer, endure or die. The path of hate and exclusion is the path of gradual self-dissipation. The path of competition is the sure way to the abyss of annihilation.

The essence of the vital force (rajas, prāna, élan) consists in inward self-gathering, self-centering, increasing self-organization and structural complexification. This gives rise to Nature's evolutionary process and man's historical order. The creative flow of evolution running through cosmic Nature is conditioned by increasing complexification of structure accompanied by corresponding simplification of function and behavior. The truth of this observation is exemplified even in such primordial energy structures as electrons, protons, atoms, molecules, cells, cellular societies, etc.

The one remarkable offshoot of this self-centering and self-structuring of energy is the creative emergence at critical moments of higher and higher qualities, functions, values and levels of being. For instance, when such divergent molecules as carbon, hydrogen, oxygen, nitrogen, etc., combine in definite proportions, a qualitative novelty, a unique and unprecedented modality of being, namely the living cell, is born. It shows the emergent ability for such new functions as spontaneous mobility, immanent growth from within, self-reparation, self-regulation, self-reproduction, etc. This is known in modern philosophy as the law of emergent or creative evolution. This law represents a higher synthesis in which the religious theory of creation out of nothing and the Darwinian theory of mechanistic evolution through natural selection are harmonized. In the course of evolution, new forms, new qualities, new values continually emerge into being.[4] Life evolved out of the abysmal depths of matter; animal sentience evolved out of the impetus of life; man's rational self-consciousness evolved out of the spiraling matrix of animal sentience. In the course of the creative advance of human evolution we know that god-like men, illumined persons endowed with cosmic truth-vision, evolve through prodigious centralization of consciousness. In yoga philosophy this is known as the Law of Tapas-Sristi. This means that when a person by virtue of long practice of intelligent and purposive self-organization (Brahmacharya) generates the internal psychic heat of creative spiritual energy (Tapas),[5] then new visions of truth, beauty, and perfection illuminate his mental horizon and transform his total being into a channel of creativity. Herein lies the secret of original creativity of all such masterminds as Buddha, Krishna, Christ, Moses, Mohammed, Zoroaster, Lao-tze, and the like.

According to a Hindu legend, at the beginning of a new cycle of creation, the creator Brahmā was wondering what kind of fresh novelty he could produce this time. Suddenly he heard a voice from the void, declaring loud and clear: "Tapas, Tapas, Tapas," which means: "Go into the depth of your being, marshal all energy toward the center, and generate the internal heat of new creativity." It is this heat and flame of creativity which is variously known as the mystic fire, the splendor of inner lightening, the pure flame of divine love; the kundalini.

In our human life if we take to heart this principle of novel creation and develop a life style of self-centering and sincere dedication to some such supreme value as truth, beauty, goodness, perfection, peace, freedom and the like, then we are launched upon the path of increasing spiritual unfoldment. Self-development brings in an increasing measure the divine blessings of expanding knowledge, broadening compassion, intrinsic joy, and illumined action. We see here the law of Karma operative on the evolutionary level. Viewed from the evolutionary perspective, the law of karma may then be stated somewhat as follows:

The more you intensify your consciousness in search

of the true Self or the ultimate meaning of life, the more you gain access to unexpected treasures of the spirit.

The Law of Karma on the Cosmic Level

The inner evolutionary process eventually leads one to the cosmic vision of truth suffused with the sweetness of love and compassion. Revealed to the eye of cosmic vision is the essential structure of the cosmic whole as an all-encompassing, self-coherent system, which is self-adjusting, self-regulating and self-manifesting. Cosmic balance and harmony is the name of its essential form.

Viewed from different standpoints the cosmic balance acquires different names. When we look at it from the standpoint of intellect or reason, the cosmic balance appears as the rational structure of the universe or as the system of all systems. Herein lies the fundamental faith of the scientist and the philosopher. This faith consists, as Albert Einstein puts it, in "profound reverence for the rationality made manifest in existence." The more the scientist contemplates the operation of laws in nature, the more he is inspired with a religious attitude of awe and humility "towards the grandeur of reason incarnate in existence."[6]

It is by the way of developing the same attitude that the systems view[7] of the universe has evolved in contemporary scientific thought. From the philosophical viewpoint then the highest law of the universe, the supreme and eternal law (Dharma), appears as perfect self-consistency (Satyam). The world's various philosophical schools (darśanas) try to articulate this cosmic self-coherence in various conceptual frameworks.

The fundamental laws of science, such as the law of conservation of energy, and that of cause and effect, are expressions of the eternal Dharma on the scientific level. They may be said to constitute the intellectual aspect of the Law of Karma. In other words, from the intellectual standpoint, the Law of Karma means that nothing happens in this world without a definite cause. It follows that we can control any special kind of happening by suitably changing its cause. If for instance we know the cause of a particular kind of suffering, we can eliminate that suffering by rooting out its cause.

Viewed from the esthetic standpoint, the cosmic balance appears as the harmony of multitudinous sense-impressions. The human mind experiences this harmony of sensations as the beautiful (Sundaram). Since both the true and the beautiful are modes of expression of the spirit of harmony, they are certainly very akin to each other.

Viewed from the standpoint of volition and action, the universe as a self-coherent and self-adjusting system appears as an inviolable ethical order (Sivam). Our practical reason or moral sense perceives in the cosmic harmony an active principle of cosmic justice (Ritam, Bhadram, Subham) controlling the operations of Nature and the destinies of man.[8] Herein lies the specific meaning of the Law of Karma, as ordinarily understood—our faith in the moral structure of the universe. Moral faith can be formulated thus: as you sow, so you reap; like action, like consequence (jeman karma teman phal). Mahatma Gandhi laid special stress upon this implication of the Law of Karma: violence begets violence, hatred begets hatred, so love alone can lift man from the self-destructive vicious circle of mutual negativity.

Another way the Law of Karma can be expressed is: "He who lives by the sword, perishes by the sword"; conversely, he who lives in the love of truth shines on the lotus of love. Whereas he who thrives on greed perishes in the mud, he who delights in self-giving for the good of others, receives the blessings of God in abundant measure.

In the biological sphere, the Law of Karma assumes the form of ecological balance. The quality of life degenerates if the proper balance is not maintained in the interrelationship of various life forms and in the interaction between life and the physical environment. Violation of this law in the shape of indiscriminate commercial exploitation of the precious resources of Nature has brought us today to the verge of serious ecological crisis. Mother Nature is warning us to the effect: control your greed, or perish.

In the sphere of international relations the Law of Karma is revealed in terms of the balance of power and justice. This means that military power should be employed in international politics only as a handmaid to international justice. Otherwise it is bound to prove self-destructive and internecine.

Unfortunately, at our present stage of evolution, there is a tragic divorce, a yawning chasm, between political power and ethical justice. Until and unless this gulf is bridged by bringing sanity into the sphere of political action the chances of abiding world peace are very slim indeed.

Thus it is the spirit of balance and harmony which sustains the universe in its proper course. Without the force of balance (sattva) holding sway over the opposite forces of tamas and rajas, matter and life, outward self-expansion and inward self-organization, the universe would cease to be the cosmic order that it is. It is the spirit of harmony that creatively holds together the disintegrating entropy of matter and the evolutionary negentropy of life. In consequence, the evolutionary process in man continuously advances toward higher and higher levels of consciousness—toward the heavenly boons of immortality (amiritam), truth, love and beauty (satyam, śivam, sundaram).

It is thus the law of harmony which constitutes the ultimate foundation of both science and religion. On

the one hand it guarantees the conservation of all
energy which is the cornerstone of science; on the other
it guarantees the conservation of all values which is the
cornerstone of ethics and religion. By harmonizing
seemingly conflicting forces such as matter and life,
nature and spirit, body and mind, existence and essence, fact and value, it provides the right kind of environment within which the process of creative evolution
may go on and the precious fruits thereof be duly pre-
served.

On the cosmic scale, the spirit of balance (sattva)
makes our universe a self-maintaining, self-adjusting,
self-regulating system. Instead of an amorphous mass
of chaos and confusion it is a self-coherent whole. This
basic structural feature of the universe is personified in
Hindu philosophy in the image of Lord Vishnu, the
supreme God of harmony and love. He is associated
with two seemingly conflicting symbols: the infinite
serpent (Ananta) and the Sun-bird (Garuda).[9] This
bears a striking resemblance to the image of
Zarathustra whose two animal companions were, as
Nietzsche points out, the serpent and the eagle. The
serpent symbolizes the vital energy, the unconscious
instinctual drive (libido), which has a tendency to dissipate itself in extroversion. But the same energy is also
capable of being rechanneled in an entirely different
direction—upward.

The sun-bird garuda is the symbol of the power of
spirit. It is the spirit of freedom in upward evolution
which transforms instinctual energy and carries it upward on the sunlit path toward the thousand-petalled
blossoming of man's divine potential (Kundalini). This
upward evolutionary movement is triggered by the in-
gathering and inwardly focussing concentration of consciousness (pratyāhāra, dhāraṇa and dhyāna) oriented
to the ultimate goal of life.

The Convergence of Science and Mysticism

It is an exciting development of our present time that modern science, as a result of its recent revolutionary discoveries, has come very close to the eternal truths of mysticism. Contemporary science, following the lead of Einstein and Planck, has rejected the atomistic, mechanistic, and reductionistic outlook of older scientists. It is developing a systemic world view of enormous significance. Implicit in this development is a perfect reversal of outlook revealing the cosmic manifold as the diversification of one unified field of energy.

Bringing together the laws of science and the truths of mysticism, Integral Philosophy contemplates the cosmic whole as a superorganic unity and self-harmonizing system of divergent forces imperceptibly jostling and blending with one another within the limits of an all-controlling order (eternal dharma). Integral Yoga, which is the practical application of the integral world view, lays its major emphasis upon the need for total integration of personality with a view to perfecting the art of harmonious living in tune with the creative urge of Being (Brahman).[10]

Let us now turn to a brief consideration of the implication of the law of karma in regard to the trend of human self-development. Man holds in the depth of his being a profound spiritual potential, a divine spark for endless perfectibility. This is his *swadharma,* his distinctive human essence. The law of cosmic balance (viswa dharma) that we mentioned before maintains the dynamic and evolutionary balance of life by harmonizing opposite forces such as matter and life, devolution and evolution, regress and progress. In our human life the two most fundamental dynamic forces are *karma* and *swadharma,* the conative thrust of the past and the developmental attraction of the future, the drive of desire embodied in samskāra and the dream of self-perfection embodied in spiritual aspiration (āsprihā, sankalpa).

In other words, all our dynamic thinking oriented to the future is the result of constant interaction between the forces of the past and the future, between *karma* and *swadharma,* between samskāra and sankalpa, between the will to live and enjoy, and the will to love and be one with Being. To put it in still other words, the dynamics of our self-unfoldment are the result of active interplay between the unseen force of past actions (adrista) and the free initiative for higher development (purusakāra), between the force of past history and the light of potential liberation (moksa).

The more our knowledge expands, the more we learn to make a judicious adjustment between the karmic dynamism of the past and the creative urge of our inner potential oriented to the future. The motivations flowing from such interaction ultimately determine our course of evolution.

Be it noted here in passing that Karma does not mean any external coercive agency. It does not mean the kind of supernatural fate which was illustrated in the tragic dramas of the ancient Greeks. Nor does it mean any arbitrary fiat or predetermined command of the divine will (kismet). That would be a violation of the ethical order of life (Ritam) which the Law of Karma presupposes.

Be it also noted that true freedom does not mean absolutely arbitrary action or irrational choice which some modern existentialist philosophers eulogize. Rightly understood, freedom means our ability to act and live in the light of our own human essence (swadharma), the inner light revealing the purpose of our being as a unique mode of manifestation of Being, a distinctive creative center of the cosmic whole (Brahman, Pūrnam).

In an attempt to actualize the spiritual potential,

some mystics aspire for immortality after death on the supernatural plane. If they follow the right path, they surely can attain such supernatural self-fulfillment. The Bhakti Yoga tradition of India,[11] as well as the currents of devotional mysticism flowing through Judaism, Christianity and Sufism, emphasize this Karmic connection between authentic divine love and rapturous communion with God, the supernatural Lord of the universe.

Some spiritual seekers focus the deep longing of their hearts upon blissful union with transcendent Being, the eternal Spirit or indeterminable Godhead beyond God. This is especially emphasized in the contemplative approach of the Yoga of Knowledge in India,[12] and in the mystical traditions of Plato and Plotinus, Jacob Boehme and Meister Eckhart, Jalal Uddin Rumi and pseudo-Dionysius and others.

It should be noted here that the Theosophical Movement has rendered a signal service to sincere spiritual seekers all over the world by laying stress upon the validity of all the major religious and spiritual paths as means of ultimate spiritual fulfillment.

Integral Yoga shares with Theosophy this universality of spiritual outlook. Its special emphasis is geared to the evolutionary potentials of the emerging New Age—the Supramental Age. A suitable integration of the future-oriented spiritual values in the world's major mystical traditions is the dominant keynote of this new yoga dedicated to the outflowering of the Divine in global humanity.

The Karmic significance of Integral Yoga is that if we learn how to consciously cooperate with the creative force of planetary evolution as it is shaping up with the passage of time, mankind's age-old dream of the kingdom of heaven on earth, i.e., an internationally unified world order controlled by the power of truth, justice and love, can inevitably come true.

So the focus of integral self-discipline does not lie on mystic self-realization, whether on the supernatural level or on the transcendental level. Its focus is rather on the paramount desirability of harmonizing the mystic realization with the evolutionary perspective as well as the individuated self-discovery. United with the eternal, the integrated individual would joyfully cooperate with the process of evolution toward the emergence of a new global society.[13]

References

[1] Haridas Chaudhuri, *Being, Evolution & Immortality*. Wheaton, Illinois: Quest Books, 1974.

[2] Ibid, Ch. VII.

[3] Isaac Asimov, *The New Intelligent Man's Guide to Science*. New York: Basic Books, 1965. p. 328.

[4] Samuel Alexander, *Space, Time, and Deity*. Vol. I. London: George Allen & Unwin.

[5] S. Radhakrishnan, *The Principal Upanishads*. New York: Harper, 1953. p. 253-54.

[6] Albert Einstein, *Out of My Later Years*. New York: Wisdom Library, a division of Philosophical Library, 1950. P. 33.

[7] Ervin Laszlo, *The Systems View of the World*. New York: George Braziller, 1972.

[8] S. Chatterjee & Datta, *An Introduction to Indian Philosophy*. Calcutta: University of Calcutta, 1950. p. 14-15.

[9] Heinrich Zimmer, *Myths and Symbols in Indian Art & Civilization*. New York: Pantheon Books, 1947. p. 76.

[10] Haridas Chaudhuri, *Integral Yoga: The Concept of Harmonious and Creative Living*. Wheaton, Illinois: Quest Books, 1974. Ch. 1.

[11] Ibid, pp. 67-71.

[12] Ibid, pp. 62-66.

[13] Ibid, pp. 51-52, 81-82.

10.

The Side Blows of Karma

Some Thoughts on the Outworking of Karma
GEORGE E. LINTON

> ". . . you know nothing of the *ins* and outs of the work
> of Karma—of the 'side blows' of this terrible law."[1]

The quotation is from a letter to Mr. A. P. Sinnett,
received by him in London in 1884, from the Mahatma
Koot Hoomi. The Mahatma is discussing with Sinnett
the failure of an endeavor to establish in India a news-
paper under the latter's management. The previous
year, the owners of the Allahabad *Pioneer* had termi-
nated Sinnett's editorship of that paper, and he and his
friends had been endeavoring to raise sufficient funds
from the Indians to start a new paper which would be
sympathetic to the Indian viewpoint. The endeavor had
failed, due to the lack of support by the Indian finan-
ciers. The Mahatma asks Sinnett if he ever had any idea
as to the *real reason* why the venture had failed, and then
he intimates that it was a karmic "side blow" occasioned
by the fact that in his earlier years in India, Sinnett had
looked upon the Indians as an inferior race and had felt
a profound contempt for them at that time. So at this
later date, when he wanted to help the Indians and
could have done much useful work for their better-
ment, his past karma denied him the opportunity.

The short study which follows is an endeavor to
consider some of the ways in which karma appears to
operate, based on information which is available, together with some added observations. Many events

occur which to our limited observation are seemingly accidental or without adequate explanation; some are pleasant and some are tragic. Yet if we could see the entire picture, we would probably find that they are all the direct or indirect results of past actions, emotions, or thoughts. Take for example the large number of fatalities that occur each year on our highways. From a superficial point of view, there appears to be no logical moral reason why a particular accident occurs at a particular time and place, involving certain specific individuals. There is no apparent reason why "X" should be the one to run into "Y," a total stranger, and kill him. But perhaps they are not such total strangers as it appears at first thought. This is where the theory of reincarnation comes into the picture and adds the missing parts of the story which enable one to see that there may be some link that will explain the reason for this partic ar "accident." Perhaps the two entities who are the real beings who are at the present time functioning on the physical plane as "X" and "Y" have met before, in some previous incarnation; perhaps "X" is settling some past action in which "Y" has been involved and has to account for. But whatever the reason, there must have been some antecedent cause for the occurrence if one is to believe in a moral law of universal justice operating in the world. To the occultist, nothing can happen by accident.

Or again, some chance meeting may bring about a life-long friendship or some other good fortune for no apparent reason. Again appearance may be deceiving, and what appears to be accidental may be really the fulfillment of some cause set in motion earlier.

First, perhaps it would be advisable to review briefly the general concept of the law of karma and how it operates. A general outline can be found in many theosophical books, so there is no need to discuss the subject at length here, but a few basic considerations may be helpful. It is considered to be a basic law in nature that when equilibrium is disturbed at any point, a corrective action must take place sooner or later to restore the balance. Since manifestation itself is an action that disturbs the equilibrium of matter in *pralaya* (the state of rest in which it exists during periods of inactivity), nature is ever in the process of restoring balances, hence it is stated that karma is action (implying also reaction). Ceaseless eternal motion is the order of the universe, states one of the Mahatmas in a letter to Mr. Sinnett, and affinity or attraction its handmaid of all work.[2]

If karma is a universal law in nature, its operation should and must follow (ultimately) a lawful pattern, and therefore if all the facts regarding a relationship are known it should be possible to accurately predict the results that will follow. In other words, a proper understanding of the law of cause and effect at all levels of being should enable one so to order his life that certain definite results will ensue. In general, however, few people stop to consider the underlying causes of many of the things that happen to them, being content to attribute these to circumstances, chance, or fate. They are content to deal with results rather than to seek for basic causes and deal with these causes. Life in the western world today is so busy and hectic that few take the necessary time to analyze things and find out the why of them. In fact, few would be willing to admit that they are living and operating within moral and spiritual energy fields, the laws governing which are as unerring, impersonal, and predictable as the laws governing the gravitational and electromagnetic fields. Many in fact would be loath to acknowledge that everything that happens to them is the result of actions which they themselves have set in motion at sometime in the past, either in this or in some prior incarnation.

A recognition of the existence of such moral and

ethical laws and a search for knowledge as to how best to live in accordance with them would go far toward making life more livable and would enable mankind to progress more swiftly along its evolutionary path. Instead we are content to spend much of our time and energy trying to counter effects without seeking to find the underlying causes, thus bringing upon ourselves much unnecessary trouble, as for instance when we get an acid stomach, we seek to overcome the difficulty by taking some patent medicine, rather than finding out what is wrong with our eating habits and correcting them. Or, again, we raise our taxes in order to provide treatment and care for chronic alcoholics, while at the same time spending uncounted millions of dollars promoting the sale of alcoholic beverages, thus encouraging people to become alcoholics.

The concept of a universal law of justice is a simple one in principle. It is only when we begin to apply it to specific situations that we begin to have difficulty in observing its operation. Comprehension requires an understanding of basic theosophic concepts regarding the planes of nature, the origin and purpose of life, the total constitution of man and his various vehicles of consciousness. Unless one has an understanding of the fact that man is essentially a spiritual being, rooted in an ultimate reality and expressing himself on the mental, emotional, and physical planes of nature in vehicles suitable for use on those planes throughout a long series of incarnations in these different vestures of evolutionary experiencing, one will be unable to realize that nature has laws which are operative at these higher levels with as great a degree of certainty as those which are known at the physical level. Without this knowledge of the total picture of man, the idea of karmic law will be difficult to comprehend.

According to Dr. Annie Besant, every event in our lives, at whatever level, is linked to a preceding cause, and generally also to a succeeding result, so that life appears to us to be a continuous flow of events.[3]

In many instances we can perceive, or imagine that we can, the direct action of this law of compensation or balance as it applies to an individual person, provided the balancing effect takes place within a short period of time. If the karma has been accumulated at some earlier time in the life of the person or in some previous incarnation, we are normally unable to make any reasonable connection with the current event, since the whole picture is not available to us in the ordinary conditions of consciousness; but this lack of knowledge does not preclude the existence of the chain of causative events. We are constantly in the process of generating new karma, or balancing up past actions, and the results we think of in terms of good or bad, helpful or harmful, etc. Of course, in reality there is neither good nor bad karma since these are relative terms coined by man to describe things on the basis of his own judgment. Karma in itself is without attributes of man-made morality.

The intricate network of events impinging upon an individual and producing an offsetting reaction in him might be illustrated graphically by analogy to the vector diagrams used in the analysis of mechanical forces in the study of mechanics. In these diagrams the direction of the force is indicated by the direction of the line and the strength of the force by its relative length. The composite action of a group of forces acting through a given point produces a resultant which is of a certain strength and direction. To produce a state of equilibrium, another force equal and opposite to this resultant must be applied. The analogy fits quite well if we consider the individual as the point and the external forces acting upon him from differing directions as the vectors, producing a resultant effect which we call his karma. To maintain his state of equilibrium, he must exert a force which will neutralize the external forces, otherwise he will be pushed about by them until he, willingly or unwillingly, does something to bring about the balance, i.e., until he has settled the karmic debt.

Karma can be considered under several categories such as personal karma and group karma (national, racial, religious, etc.), or by levels of causation and out-working, or by time sequence. By this last is meant such things as current, earlier in life, or in some past incarnation. It is said that karma which has been accumulated in past incarnations is apportioned to the individual in a particular lifetime by certain intelligent forces in nature (generally referred to as the *Lipika*). The special function of these forces seems to be that of maintaining the integral balance of the universe and therefore of all the separate elements within it. The methods by which this is accomplished are not easily comprehended, except possibly by those who would personalize these forces as agents of an anthromorphic God.

It is stated by some students that no one is burdened in any one lifetime with an amount of his past karma greater than he is able to bear. Some persons might question this assurance when all the "slings and arrows of outrageous fortune" that are heaped upon them seem to be too much for them to cope with; but somehow most people do seem to manage to get through life, even though it isn't always easy. This applies especially to those circumstances which appear to be mostly burdens and misfortunes. Whether or not people have the same capacity to bear excessive good fortune might be questioned, as persons in these circumstances are the ones who seem to fail most often to make the best use of their opportunities. Few indeed seem to be able to withstand the effects of excessive wealth or power without abusing the opportunities and obligations that these offer or require, and thus creating for themselves much new karma of an unfortunate kind that they will be long in working out. As one of the Indian Adepts once remarked to Mr. Sinnett, "It is only in adversity that we can discover the true man." History seems to bear out this statement as excessive affluence, either individually or as a nation, is usually followed in a short time by decadence.

If we consider how karma works at the superphysical levels of consciousness, we need to understand how thought and emotion act and react in our lives. The matter of these planes being much more tenuous and rapid in movement than that of the dense physical, it is natural to expect that actions and reactions will occur with greater suddenness and rapidity at those levels. Tensions and disturbances in the emotional and mental planes can discharge themselves suddenly and with violence, as can an electrical discharge or the elements in a thunderstorm.

When the psychic atmosphere thus erupts, we see the results often in physical form, whether natural or man-made as in the case of revolutions, mob violence, or political disturbances. When a group of people or a nation builds up vast clouds of turbulence in the psychic atmosphere, it can seldom be dissipated slowly, but generally takes the form of physical disruption and violence such as we are now witnessing in connection with racial and social problems.

The mechanics by which karmic obligations are carried forward from one incarnation to the next until they are balanced out is something that is not easy to comprehend. During the intermediate periods between incarnations, the experiences of the incarnation just completed are said to be assimilated into the Ego or spiritual nature by a process analagous to digestion, and the valuable parts of such experiences are built into the causal body, the permanent vehicle of the individual consciousness on the plane of abstract mind. The portions not suitable for absorption in the form of traits of character, capacities, talents, etc., are said to be left behind at the threshold of the heaven world, to be picked up again by the entity when it returns to incarnation at the physical level. The amount of this carry-over of unfinished business must be considerable, with humanity still at the present stage of imperfection, and so we can probably attribute many things in our lives to actions that we ourselves have generated in prior incarnations. The actual method by which these uncompleted actions (primarily of a less spiritual nature) are brought forward from incarnation to incarnation is not described in theosophical literature except in general terms, and this mostly by analogy. It is indicated that the individuality through the causal body maintains a continuing connection with the lower planes through attachments to certain particular "atoms" of those planes which perform the function of supplying vibratory or harmonic capabilities around which it attracts matter of the lower planes when reincarnating. These "atoms" collect the matter of the astral and physical planes suitable to the requirements of the individuality according to karmic law.

In Buddhist metaphysics, it is stated that the skandhas play an important part in the transmission of the "unfinished business" of one incarnation to the next. The skandhas are said to be the elements of limited existence, the "bundles of attributes" of the personal self, which are ever at work preparing the abstract mold, or "privation" of the future "new being."[4] In Buddhist philosophy these are listed as five in number, and together they make up the personal self with its sense of separate existence. While they disappear at time of death, they form the attributes of the future personality, and although there is no personal recollection of them in the new brain-mind in the ensuing incarnation, nevertheless they appear to be "forwarders" of the results of past action, in part at least. Thus when the individual returns again to the sphere of objective existence, part of the karma embodied in these privations is assumed in the new life (incarnation). The remainder presumably carries over until a still later incarnation. Perhaps we may infer that the "abstract mold" referred to attracts to itself matter of the lower planes that is harmonically attuned to its vibratory rates, and thus we get the type of physical, etheric, and emotional bodies which we deserve and to which we are entitled. "Like attracts like" as we all know, and this should be as applicable to the mental and emotional worlds as it is to the physical. The Mahatma, in another of his letters to Mr. Sinnett, asserts that "this law of attraction asserts itself in many seemingly inexplicable incidents in life, into which the entity has been drawn by the preponderating influences of past life actions."[5]

It is indicated by a number of clairvoyant investigators that the outline or characteristics of both the mental and emotional bodies are formed by or for the returning entity prior to the formation of the etheric and dense physical bodies for the projected incarnation. From this it would seem that the course the personality is to take in a particular incarnation is determined to a large extent prior to the birth of the physical body. Some investigators have indicated that some of the specific elements of this coloring process enter into the aura of the child at an early age and become diffused into the aura at the astral and lower levels. Possibly this is part of the method of operation of the skandhas of the Buddhists. The Mahatma writing to Mr. Sinnett further corroborates this point when he states that there are no "accidents of birth," as the new personality coming into incarnation is almost entirely the product of the past, and that the circumstances of the new existence have already been determined essentially by ourselves, meaning presumably our higher or spiritual selves. The cholera victim, he says, could not have died from the disease had not the "germs" for the development of the disease existed within him from birth. It would seem that the word "germs" is used here in the sense of latent causes rather than in the medical sense.

In considering further some of the ways in which karma works, it is said that physical acts to another produce reactions of a physical nature, depending in type and effect upon the motive behind the act as well as the act itself. Generosity from an unselfish motive is said to be productive of an agreeable environment in the future, whereas the same act performed from a selfish motive will not produce the same result as regards the future circumstances. Mistaken efforts to help another, performed from a good motive, will produce less reaction than if done from a poor motive, but in either case, the balance of justice must eventually be restored.[6] Deliberate cruelty, whether to man or animal, is said to result in physical impairment of some appropriate kind in a later incarnation. A person suffering from some congenital handicap or crippling disease may wonder why fate has visited such affliction on him for no reason of which he is aware in his own mind, i.e., his present brain consciousness. But perhaps if he could see behind the veil, and gain a more comprehensive view of things, he would see that he is only paying a just debt for something that he has done in some earlier incarnation. At the level of consciousness of the spiritual self, the individual is undoubtedly aware of the reasons for the presently existing situation.

Most every investigator capable of observing at the level of consciousness of the immortal self, and who can trace back the life of an entity through past incarnations, has testified that deliberate cruelty is one of the most terrible of crimes and results in the most severe karmic repayments. Some of these investigators indicate that this situation applies not alone to actions between man and man but also to man's treatment of the animal kingdom. Unintentional cruelty or cruelty from necessity do not appear to evoke the drastic karmic responses that accrue from intentional cruelty. It may be a long time before the world is free from pain and suffering, but to deliberately add to the existing accumulation is not aiding in the evolution of life on our planet.

Before leaving this point, it should be recognized that cruelty to another human being can be perpetrated at the mental and emotional levels as well as at the physical level. In fact it seems probable that some people generate more suffering and anguish among their families and friends in this manner than by physical means, and oftentimes are quite unaware of it. But regardless of the manner in which the cruelty is manifested, whether intentional or not, the law of compensation will eventually bring about suitable redress.

Neither should we overlook the other side of the ledger, since love as well as hate is a binding force; while its reactions may be much more agreeable to bear, it is still something which binds people together. As to whether this type of link is a help or a hindrance to one's evolutionary advancement is perhaps a matter for individual consideration. Both are creators of karmic ties, and eventually it would seem that a time must come in one's stage of evolution when one should not be bound by either. Action without desire for the results of the action has ever been the attitude of the seeker after liberation from the bondage of the personal self, an attitude ably set forth in the Hindu classic, the *Bhagavad Gita.*

The collective karma of a group or a nation is something to which we probably give much less thought than to our individual karma. This is perhaps due in part to the fact that it is less observable and not as easily understood as our personal situation. The greater the freedom of the individual and the better the educational level, the greater the opportunity to become involved with the larger units of society and thus participate in the collective karma of the nation or group. In times past, when communication was limited—and even in some underdeveloped countries today—interest was and is centered more at the family and group level, and probably the collective karma was much less than in the Western nations of the world today with the world-wide contacts, communication, business problems, and political differences which exist. A public generally enlightened about events on a global scale, with all the problems involved between nations and cultures, must be creating a vast amount of collective karma, not only physically but also emotionally and mentally. Moral and ethical conduct by a nation becomes more and more a responsibility of the individuals in that nation. Considering the violent thoughts and feelings, mostly of a negative kind, which are being aroused both within the nations and on a global scale, the psychic atmosphere of the world today must be full of turbulence and charged to the point of explosiveness. It is little wonder that we are witnessing so much violence and turmoil.

The Christian scripture admonishes us to return good for evil, and while this evokes the heart qualities in man, it still leaves him tied karmically to the recipient of his meritorious action. Return good for good, for evil, justice, says the Confucian, which would seem to be more in keeping with a philosophical approach to life. This approach would also seem to be more in keeping with the teachings of the Lord Krishna as given in the *Bhagavad Gita,* where a more impersonal attitude toward the results of one's actions is advised.

Justice "makes no difference between the many and the few," says the previously quoted Mahatma,[7] which would seem to indicate that the integrity of a nation or a social group is just as important as one's personal integrity, and that all alike are weighed in the scales of justice. But how often do we find complete honesty and true integrity in the field of international diplomacy, or even in the business world? It would seem that the individual citizen should be as much concerned with the honesty and integrity of his country as he is in his own personal life, for in the end he has to assume accountability for both.

The subject of group karma has some very interesting aspects which deserve consideration by the individual who is striving to live in accordance with his highest understanding. In everyday life, how little thought is given to the karmic aspects of one's group associations or of professions of which one makes use. Does one ever consider that in belonging to a religion or in availing oneself of the services of the medical profession, as examples, one is partaking to some extent in the collective karma of these groups? In joining a religion, does the devotee ever consider his vicarious association with the intolerance and persecution which have been perpetrated by that sect? Does the person who avails himself of the latest developments in medical practice ever stop to think of the suffering and torture that may have accompanied the development of those techniques? Probably not, but it is something deserving serious thought.

As long as minds and emotions continue to generate hatred, jealousy, envy, and greed, whether as individuals or as members of a group, so long will karmic ties be created and karmic debts be balanced out. When will the wheel stop turning? Who knows? But probably not until all of mankind has reached perfection.

References

[1] *The Mahatma Letters to A. P. Sinnett,* transcribed and compiled by A. T. Barker, 3rd ed., Adyar: Theosophical Publishing House, 1962, p. 347.
[2] Ibid., p. 67.
[3] Annie Besant, *The Ancient Wisdom,* Adyar: Theosophical Publishing House, p. 272.

[4] Barker, op cit., p. 109.
[5] Ibid., p. 147.
[6] Besant, op cit., p. 286.
[7] Barker, op cit., p. 395.

11.

The Other Face of Karma

VIRGINIA HANSON

Few people who have given serious thought to the subject of karma would deny that it is one of the most complex, the most profound, and probably the least understood of all the great universal principles expounded in the lieerature of Theosophy. To attempt to touch upon any of its more subtle aspects may seem presumptuous in the extreme. In particular, as one approaches the subject from a Christian background, one may seem to be inviting an impasse, for sooner or later he is confronted with the juxtaposition of karma as an immutable law and grace with its secret and mysterious dynamics which seem to operate independently of law.

In human affairs, both karma and grace may, in a sense, be said to "happen," that is, they are experienced and experienceable. This seems undeniable fact, so that neither can be denied. We feel instinctively that fact cannot be untruth; at the same time, it can never be the whole of truth. It says, in effect, "I am both hiding and revealing truth." Dare one explore what is hidden beneath what is revealed in the action of karma and grace?

The mere placing of these two words together may seem to be drawing lines for an irresolvable conflict. In the dead-letter, literal interpretation of karma as a mechanical process grinding on and on like a locomotive on a single pair of tracks, there can be no such thing as grace. In the sentimental, wishful, unrealistic view of grace as a favor dispensed by a jealous and erratic God, to be gained by flattery and profession of belief, karma is a concept to be rejected vehemently. Yet in any real and earnest search for truth there can be no conflict, for the searcher does not begin with rejection; he does not begin with any conditioned attitude at all, but only with eyes and mind open to see what he may find.

What is the nature of the reality of karma? What is the nature of the reality of grace? And what is the nature of the relationship between them? Are they two sides of a coin, or are they totally foreign and antagonistic to each other?

H.P. Blavatsky calls karma "the One Law which governs the World of Being."[1] It has been described as the Absolute in the process of manifestation and as manifestation seeking to restore the harmony of the Absolute. It is spoken of as impersonal, inexorable, immutable—but also as modifiable. It has been called a "mathematical equation."

Sir James Jeans, the British scientist, declared that "the universe appears to have been designed by a pure mathematician"[2] and that ". . . the laws which nature obeys are less suggestive of those which a machine obeys in its motion than of those which a musician obeys in writing a fugue, or a poet in composing a sonnet. The motions of electrons and atoms do not resemble those of the parts of a locomotive so much as those of the dancers in a cotillion."[3] In other words, they seem volitional rather than automatic; they are dependable and observable, yet they hold forever the potential of creative innovation. But, mysteriously, the innovation never creates confusion; rather it seems to grow logically out of the inner meaning of the dance. Such steps as are no longer appropriate become transformed into that which is useful to an ever-expanding synthesis.

In his book, *Out of My Later Years,* Albert Einstein comments on the element of unpredictability in atomic behavior and adds: "One need only think of the weather, in which case accurate prediction even for a few days ahead is impossible. Nevertheless, no one doubts that we are confronted with a causal connection. Occurrences in this domain are beyond the reach of exact prediction because of the variety of factors in operation, not because of any lack of order in nature."[4]

In other words, the creative innovations of nature do not mean breaches of law. They simply mean that the law has so many variables within it that no one can say he has final and conclusive knowledge of all its workings.

So we have a concept of a great mathematician whose nature is law, but with untold reserves of ways in which the law may work out. Even here on our mundane plane of operations, with our limited intellects, it is a commonly known mathematical principle that when we change the relation of the elements within an equation, we change the results. As very simple examples, we can add and get one result; we can subtract, multiply, divide, square a number and carry the process to the nth power; we can extract square root, cube root, and so on; or we may introduce some new element into the equation. In all these ways we get different results. The equation must work out according to mathematical law, but the elements introduced and the relationships in which those elements are arranged determine the nature of the equation itself and what the results will be. It is known also that the solution to any equation, to any mathematical problem, always lies within the problem itself, never outside, although we may find ourselves unable to solve a problem because we are overlooking some element; we are not seeing it whole.

Surely the relationships between the myriad elements of life affect each other and the end results in any situation, in any experience, just as do the elements within a mathematical equation. The law itself makes no exception, but it would be staggeringly brash to say that we know what all the elements are or that we can predict everything that can happen within the operation of the law, particularly since no situation, no experience, is ever exactly duplicated. Although there is but One Law, it has so many facets, so many variables, that it seems to be many laws in operation; and at times we may not even be able to discern law at all because it is operating at a level far beyond our comprehension.

So it would seem that the *mechanical* explanation of karma hardly explains what is taking place. It is particularly inadequate, and holds no key to growth and understanding, if we use it *merely* as an explanation and search no deeper, in ourselves and in nature, for causes—for those elements which will make the problem whole and thus reveal its true nature.

As karma operates in our own lives, it is undoubtedly the law through which we inherit our own past. But, again, there is a hint of something deeper and more profound. The universe turns as one (which is the root meaning of the word "universe") and we all live in one element. Out of this emerges the principle of relativity. Every part of the universe must therefore be kept, at every moment, in harmony with its own integral balance. This happens, it is suggested, not only at the physical level, but at higher energy levels which are inconceivable to us. We might think of it as a "making perfect" process—or perhaps a more descriptive term would be the invincible divine will to perfection eternally in action. This gets away from the idea of something static and motionless or of something wholly mechanical. Rather it would seem to be perfect rhythm and perfect harmony, or balance, in simultaneity. The will to perfection is conceived of as the Logoic Will, and its operation in maintaining the equilibrium of the universe is, one might say, stretched out in time and space. This might be termed universal or cosmic karma.

As this applies to the individual, it is a mystical energy of inconceivable power which derives from the Logoic

Will, is one with it and is—at every moment—in rhythmic balance at the level of the Self. Disturbances (pleasant or unpleasant) take place in the outer circumstances where the fragment, the personality, is focused. The impact of these disturbances is felt—or perhaps a better term is "absorbed"—at the causal level.* But here it does not disturb the integrity and equilibrium because all is immediate and whole; no element is missing, so that everything *is* balanced and perfect at every moment. Perhaps what takes place is a perfectly coordinated operation of centrifugal and centripetal forces at every level of energy. At the mundane level, the action is slowed down so that, to us, it "takes time." It becomes our world experience. At the causal level it is instantaneous.

Events as cause and effect in space and time, then, must be worked out in the personality. And while the personality cannot escape its responsibility, it would seem that the Ego is the primary "mover." One might even go so far as to suggest the possibility that the Ego initiates the events, that is, it uses the law as a tool for its own growth, for it can develop its powers only through learning to deal with circumstances at the outpost of consciousness which we call the personality.

A concept emerging in depth psychology seems to relate to this possibility. Dr. Edward C. Whitmont comments that it has been customary in his profession to assume that traumatic experiences which might be avoided under "ideal" circumstances are responsible for the later development of neuroses or psychoses. He suggests that it may be of value to examine this assumption, and he advances the theory that these often un-

*So called in theosophical literature because it is the level where causes are "stored"—not, of course, in terms of space, but in terms of what might be called vibratory possibilities; here it is said, is distilled the essence of all experience gained by the Ego through its many incarnations. It should be noted also that the term "Ego" as used in theosophical literature does not correspond to the ego of the modern psychology, but more accurately relates to the center of consciousness called in depth psychology the Self.

happy experiences "may perhaps be seen as essential landmarks in the actualization of a pattern of whole-ness. They may be understood as the 'suffering of the soul' which is needed to engender present and future psychological advance. . . .In following the develop-ment of past events into future consequences, we might discover a meaning beyond mere cause and effect in the way the past comes to view when regarded as the first stage and necessary setting for present and future un-foldment." It may be seen, he says, "not just as accident or misfortune, but as a destined emotional impasse essential for the actualization of our own particular pattern of wholeness."[5]

Drawing a parallel with the development of the action in a drama—using the concept of Greek tragedy as a "mirror of the soul"—Dr. Whitmont points out that the sequence of events on the stage works out as cause and effect, but he adds: ". . .while it is true that the staging of the tragic or joyful situation in act two seems to be caused by the 'right' or 'wrong' action which preceded it in act one, it is equally true that this effect of causation is deliberate or destined. Act one has set the scene and built up its consequences or 'effects' in order to reveal the intent or plot of the drama as it unfolds later in actuality. . . .Although we may understand the play (as) the sequence of cause and effect, unless we are also able to comprehend the dramatic intent or the destined meaning behind the causal sequence, we will not be moved by the inner logic of its timing. . ."[6] He is making the point that there is an "archetypal destiny" for each individual which is known to the Self and that, while cause and effect are necessary to the outworking of this destiny, the real impulse comes from a much deeper level. This is not determinism, nor does it absolve the personality from its responsibility; it does not preclude the concept of free will. It is the "meaning" of the drama that is destined and must, in some act, be fulfilled. The

Ego is indeed the true Actor and the personality is the role through which he deals with the effects of his self-initiated causes. But the Actor *becomes* the role, else it is empty of meaning; it is an extension of himself onto the stage of life. The personality may choose whether to accept this fact and thus move toward the fulfillment of the meaning, or whether to delay that fulfillment by refusing to acknowledge the true nature of the drama.

All this carries the clear implication that what happens to us happens by the secret will of our own innermost being. For the Ego is not separate from the Self (using the word in the theosophical sense); it is indeed that aspect of the Self through which action must take place. In the earlier stages of evolution, this is perhaps a feeble and even fumbling process. But as the Ego develops its capacities and becomes more facile in using them, it comes more and more to direct the process and even to pose for itself greater challenges out of the inexhaustible storehouse of past experience.

Thus, we are always in the process of creating our own drama, our own world action, from within. This creation, which in its outer aspect becomes cause and effect in continual adjustment to the interrelation or interaction between the personality and its environment, is what we ordinarily think of as karma. And because, as personalities, we are mostly unaware that, as Egos, we have brought it all about, even the causes seem to impinge on us from the outside. But surely these can no more be outside ourselves than we can be outside our own hearts and minds. The causes are within us, and so long as they remain they must continually create effects.

Once a disturbance has taken place, it may take time for the balance, the harmony, to be achieved in the outer circumstances. We may even have to wait for act three or even later (here for the moment considering acts as successive incarnations) before the event in act one finds its outworking. As personalities we experience sequentially. But to the Self, the concepts of time and space must be irrelevant. "When" the impulse from the Self comes into our lives, then, it seems from our point of view to come in time and space. But what we experience as adjustment in the personality is part of the archetypal "plot," which is already perfect, whole, at the causal level; it has never been anything but perfect and whole.

The Self is not subject to the working out of personal causality because it is not subject to the personality, although, paradoxically—to take some liberty with Dr. Whitmont's hypothesis—the acting-out on the stage and the underlying theme of the drama "are not mutually exclusive but complementary and mutually in need of each other."[7] But the Self *is* harmony, integrity, perfection. Personal karma cannot affect it, however rigidly and inflexibly it may operate in the space-time world of our everyday experience. It has been pointed out that just as the sky's nature remains the same however black the clouds which pass across it, so the Self's purity is undisturbed by the human thoughts, emotions, and passions which move within its projection, the personality—although in some mysterious manner it descends into the depths with us and teaches us the meaning of the heavenly agony. But we have to remember that, even in this, the Self is still experiencing itself when it sees the myriad personal lives through which it manifests. And since it is perfection, it *experiences* only perfection. This is poetically expressed in the words, "Of purer eyes than to behold evil." Unfortunately, such concepts are too subtle for the blundering uses of language. We are constantly faced with the fact that words are indeed, as someone has called them, the broken wreckage of the reality of thought.

Quite tentatively, then, and at the risk of being misunderstood, it might be said that the Self "cares" beyond measure what happens to the personality, but because it is love in the ultimate it is not "concerned." Worry is a vice which belongs exclusively to the personality, in which love is incomplete and which is therefore insecure.

In this view, presumably, everything is "right," and when we see that which we regard as wrong or evil and attempt to remedy it, that is a part of the rightness. In this view, too, life has a kind of "built-in" integrity and immortality. Everything has an inner balance and truth and harmony; everything, in its true nature, reflects that perfect equilibrium at the core of all creation.

It seems possible, then, that this built-in integrity and immortality can be equated with the element of redemption which has received so much emphasis in the Christian religion and without which, perhaps, no resolution of karma is possible. Redemption, in this view, is not to be thought of as coming about through the sacrifice of God in the person of one son, but mystically through the Logoic sacrifice on the cross of matter, redeeming matter (which seems to resist but in reality is ever "seeking" to be redeemed), the process repeated endlessly, down to the lowliest cells and atoms of our bodies.

The symbol of the cross is of course a universal one, far antedating the Christian era. We find the conception that at the "beginning of time"—that is, of manifestation—the Logos impressed Itself upon creation in the form of a cross, the pattern of all manfestation, repeated at every level. Therefore the symbol implies, if we look deeply enough, that our efforts are divine efforts unrecognized. Or, perhaps more accurately, the cross is a symbol of the mutual sacrifice of spirit and matter in becoming one. It is not, in its profounder meaning, a symbol of death, even death as sacrifice, but of the union of opposites—God and man in mutual and simultaneous self-surrender. In every kind of cross known there is a point at which the perpendicular and horizontal shafts become indistinguishable—where they are not opposites at all, each being completely "lost" in the other. This point is at the very heart of the cross. It is what makes the symbol a cross and not some other figure. It is what makes the cross a triumph and not a disaster. It is the pattern throughout life, and it is the inner secret of redemption. Because of it, grace is a reality.

Grace, then, is not something that comes "unearned"; rather is the earning something quite different from what we think it is. It is perhaps not earning at all in the sense of achieving some reward as a result of conscious effort. Grace is unpredictable; it cannot be commanded; it operates when it will and as it will and often in ways which may seem strange to us.

In the Biblical story of Joseph, the beloved son who was sold by his jealous brothers into slavery in Egypt, there is a curious statement. It will be recalled that, after his betrayal, Joseph rose from his humble status as a slave to that of the most powerful man in Egypt, second only to Pharoah himself. He was able to interpret Pharoah's dream and to save the country from starvation during the long famine which visited the land. When Joseph's brothers came to Egypt for help, and when he finally made known to them his identity, they were profoundly afraid, for now, they thought, he would revenge himself upon them. But Joseph reassured them and added, "Ye thought evil against me; but God meant it unto good."[8] Thus was grace operating unseen through even a perfidious act. The story of Joseph, whether or not rooted in history, is a marvelous allegory of the universal grace operating in nature and which, we would say, forever makes good come out of evil.

In his book, *The Hero With a Thousand Faces,* Joseph Campbell tells the story of Virachocha, a great divinity of prehistoric Peru: "His tiara is the sun; he grasps the thunderbolt in either hand; and from his eyes descend, in the form of tears, the rains that refresh the life of the valleys of the world. . . .The meaning is that the grace that pours into the universe through the sun door is the same as the energy of the bolt that annihilates and is itself indestructible; the delusion-shattering light of the Imperishable is the same as the light that creates."[9] Is this not saying, in effect, that karma and grace, are, in fact, but two aspects of the same law?

Is it not possible that the ultimate resolution of karma is not through an extension of good deeds on the part of man, not even through detachment from the fruits of action, but mysteriously through participation in a sovereign state of being in which attachment is meaningless—a total union of the actor with the power that moves him to action, a total surrender of self and a simultaneous Self-surrender in an act of grace, the sublime and heavenly gift. The mystical energy which is the will to perfection eternally in operation "moves out" into the personality. This comes inevitably like a "visitation from on high." It is experienced within, yet it *seems* to the personality to come from *outside* because the personality has been isolated in its own zone of awareness. In other words, the Christian would say it comes from God—a God who is generally thought of as completely outside His creation. It is unexpected; it is unpredictable; and it seems totally undeserved.

This "undeserved" aspect is probably because the full flow of grace comes usually—although not always—when the self has been completely surrendered; it comes to the humble and the contrite heart, repentant and earnestly seeking to be filled with the fire and sweetness of divinity. It is the Kingdom of Heaven which "cometh as a thief in the night." It would seem to be identical with the energy, the active will to perfection, which has been termed karma—the most dynamic, the most potent form that karma can take because it brings about the awareness, in the personality, of its real nature, that total fulfillment represented by the perfect equilibrium at the heart of the cross where God and man become one. The fulfillment is inherent in the very nature of the law itself. For its nature is ever the nature of the cross. When that realization flows into the personality it is known as grace.

Grace has its own purposes, not to be discerned or controlled by man. Not always does it wait for the surrender of the self; it sometimes forces that surrender. When this happens, it can be devastating. Paul, on the road to Damascus, was blinded by it and was three days without sight or the ability to eat or drink. Yet thereafter he preached, through persecution and trial, "Christ in you, the hope of glory."[10]

Paul spoke of being "above the law, in grace," and this is often taken to mean that in some miraculous manner we can escape the working out of the law in our personal lives. Surely one may assume that Paul was speaking of that total union with the Source of the action, that oneness *with* the law which must be dimensionless and timeless. But the individual must come back again and meet his "everyday"; he may even be faced with a particularly difficult evolutionary assignment, as was Paul. And again he is subject to the operation of the law in space and time; again he is on the stage. But there is a difference. The power of grace to alter circumstances is incalculable because it alters the personality, which is the most important element in the circumstances. The theme has come to a climax. Old causes are "blotted out" and new and powerful causes are initiated. New effects become inevitable. This may be thought of as the "forgiveness of sins."

Such forgiveness can hardly mean, however, that the world experience, the life drama of the individual, will immediately become one long sweet song, or that he will never meet the consequences of the things he has done in the past. The drama continues, but not instead of being helplessly caught in its action, the actor is participating in the denouement; he is letting the action flow through him. He meets events with an entirely different consciousness, so that they themselves become something quite different from what they would otherwise have been. It is probably not too much to say that measure of the flow of grace into his life determines the degree of strength and wisdom with which he now meets and deals with experience. "The lamp of knowledge is the perception of truth. The lamp is the passionless heart; its oil is Divine grace; the air that keeps it burning is the breeze of love that blows between man and God; and the boisterous wind from which it is protected is the desire for things perceived by sense of mind."[11] Or, as it was expressed by the 17th century mystic, Brother Lawrence: ". . .our sanctification (does not depend upon *changing* our works, but in doing that for God's sake which we commonly do for our own."[12]

As to what brings about the dynamic moment of fulfillment, that moment when the law becomes self-transformed into an act of grace, who can say? Perhaps it is a decision of the Self, that power behind the action of our individual world drama. If so, we cannot know at the personal level why that decision is taken. Perhaps it is not a "decision" at all in our understanding of the term, for choice is the burden—and the gift—of individual consciousness. Perhaps it is a "happening" that takes place when all the elements of a situation have made it inevitable. Paul Brunton calls it "a descent of the Overself into the underself's zone of awareness . . . the voice of the Overself speaking suddenly out of the cosmic silence with which we are environed." And he adds, "Because the Overself exists in every man, grace too exists potentially in every man."[13]

But I think we can say that the Overself violates no law; rather that when it moves "into the underself's zone of awareness" it is its own fulfillment.

References

1. H.P. Blavatsky, *The Secret Doctrine,* Adyar: Theosophical Publishing House, 1938, 4th ed., vol. 2, p. 359.
2. Sir James Jeans, *The Mysterious Universe,* New York: The Macmillan Co., 1930, p. 140.
3. Ibid., p. 146.
4. Albert Einstein, *Out of My Later Years,* New York: Philosophical Library, Inc., 1950, p. 28.
5. Edward C.Whitmont, M.D., "The Destiny Concept in Psychotherapy," a paper read at Zurich, Switzerland, September 1968, before the Fourth Congress of the International Association for Analytical Psychology, *Spring,* 1969, p. 74.
6. Ibid., pp. 78-9.
7. Ibid., p. 79.
8. Gen. 50:20.
9. Joseph Campbell, *The Hero With a Thousand Faces,* Bollingen Series XVII, New York: Pantheon Books, Inc., pp. 145-6.
10. Col. 1:27.
11. Commentary on verse 11, Chapter X, the *Bhagavad Gita,* tr. M. Chatterji.
12. Herman Nicholas (Brother Lawrence), *The Practice of the Presence of God,* New York: Fleming H. Revell Co., 1895, p. 16.
13. Paul Brunton, *The Wisdom of the Overself,* New York: E.P. Dutton & Co., 1969, pp. 236-7.

NOTES ON CONTRIBUTORS

LAURENCE J. BENDIT, psychiatrist, lecturer, and author, held the degrees of M.A., M.D., and B. Chir (i.e. Surgery) from Cambridge University, as well as other British medical diplomas including that of specialist in psychological medicine. Before his death in September of 1974, he made a substantial contribution to the literature of psychology and Theosophy. Among his best known works are *Self-Knowledge, a Yoga for the West, The Mirror of Life and Death* and, with his late wife, Phoebe D. Bendit, *The Psychic Sense* and *This World and That.* His writings appeared frequently in theosophical journals throughout the world.

HARIDAS CHAUDHURI is Professor of Philosophy and President of the California Institute of Asian Studies in San Francisco. He also serves as President of the Cultural Integration Fellowship, a group dedicated to the promotion of cultural understanding between East and West. He received his doctorate in philosophy from the University of Calcutta in 1947 and, before coming to the United States, he was a member of the educational service of the government of West Bengal and Chairman of the Department of Philosophy at Krishnagar College. He is the author of the Quest Books *Integral Yoga* and *Being, Evolution and Immortality.*

VIRGINIA HANSON has been on the headquarters staff of The Theosophical Society in America since April of 1962. She is editor of the official journal of that Society, *The American Theosophist,* and Senior Editor for the Theosophical Publishing House, Wheaton. Before her retirement from the United States Government service she was for a number of years Publications Editor in the United States Department of Justice. She is the author of a novel, *A*

Man Should Rejoice, and other works of fiction and of numerous nonfiction articles, including those published in theosophical journals in several countries.

FELIX LAYTON served from 1966 to 1972 as National Vice-President of The Theosophical Society in America, during which time he and Mrs. Layton were engaged in lecturing and organizing new groups for the study of Theosophy as part of the field expansion work of the Society. He was educated in England, Canada, and the United States, receiving the B.S. degree in physics at the University of Michigan and the M.A. degree at Stanford University. For a number of years he was active in educational work at the International Headquarters of The Theosophical Society in Adyar, Madras, India, serving as Principal of the Besant Theosophical School and, at a later period, as Principal of the Olcott Harijan Free Schools. He has traveled and lectured widely throughout India and other Asian countries, New Zealand, Australia, and Europe. He is the author of *Einstein's Theory in the Light of Theosophy* and, with Mrs. Layton, of *Some Basic Concepts of Theosophy* and *Theosophy: Key to Understanding.*

L.H. LESLIE-SMITH, M.C., M.A., is a graduate of Oxford. Now retired, he served for thirty-eight years on the editorial staff of *The Times,* London. He became a member of The Theosophical Society in 1936 and for many years has been on the Executive Committee of the Society in England. He served as General Secretary (President) of the Society in that country from 1965 to 1969. He is Chairman of the Theosophical Publishing House in London and of Tekels Park Estate, Ltd., the theosophical center at Camberley; he is also a member of the International General Council of The Theosophical Society.

GEORGE E. LINTON, a retired Civil Engineer, has been a student of Theosophy for over forty years and has been active in the work of The Theosophical Society during most of that time. For a number of years he was on the staff of the International Headquarters at Adyar, Madras, India, where he supervised the construction of a new building for the Adyar Library and Research Centre and served on the Executive Committee of the International Society. He has also served as President of the Portland Branch and of the Northwest Federation of The Theosophical Society in America. He has been a member of the National Board of Directors of The Theosophical Society in America since 1969 and is now resident at its National Headquarters, where he is serving as Administrative Assistant to the National President.

JOY MILLS, International Vice-President of The Theosophical Society, is a graduate of the University of Wisconsin-Milwaukee, with a B.S. degree in secondary education. She has done post-graduate work at the University of Chicago and the University of Washington. A teacher by profession, she has in recent years devoted her full time to the work of The Theosophical Society, serving as both National Vice-President and, for almost nine years, as National President of the United States Section of the Society. She is the author of *Theosophy and Psychology*, editor of the Quest Book, *The Key to Theosophy:* An Abridgement, and has had many articles published in theosophical journals throughout the world. During her presidency of The Theosophical Society in America, her unique column "Perspective" appeared regularly in the monthly journal, *The American Theosophist.*

CLARENCE R. PEDERSEN, Publications and Advertising Manager for the Theosophical Publishing House, Wheaton, has followed a business career, but his avocation has long been the study of philosophy, psychology, and, in particular, Theosophy. He has been a member of The Theosophical Society for a number of years, has served as President of both the Oak Park Branch and the Illinois-Wisconsin Federation of the Society. A thoughtful student of human nature and the problems that confront the world today he is a member of the National Committee on Universal Brotherhood and participated in the formation of "Project Brotherhood Now," a program sponsored by the Society to bring about a greater awareness of the principle of the unity of life.

JAMES S. PERKINS is a commercial artist by profession, but he has for a number of years given full time to the work of The Theosophical Society. He served as National President of The Theosophical Society in America from 1945 to 1960, and as International Vice President from 1962 to 1973. He is the author of numerous published works, his major books being *From Death to Rebirth* and *A Geometry of Space and Consciousness,* both illustrated with his own symbolic drawings and paintings. He and Mrs. Perkins are presently living at The Manor, the theosophical center in Sydney, Australia, of which he is the head.

LINA PSALTIS is particularly well known as a student of the writings of H.P. Blavatsky. She has for several years conducted study groups in Theosophy, lectured occasionally, and contributed articles to various theosophical journals. One of her outstanding contributions to theosophical literature is the Quest Book, *Dynamics of the Psychic World,* compiled, with notes, from the writings of H.P. Blavatsky on magic, mediumship, psychism, and the powers of the spirit. Mrs. Psaltis has also been closely associated with Boris de Zirkoff in compiling and editing the H.P. Blavatsky *Collected Writings.*

ARTHUR ROBSON has been a member of The Theosophical Society for many years. He was born and educated in India and, after receiving his degree, taught in several schools in that country before coming to England to live in 1955. He has been active in the English Section of the Society since that time and has made a substantial contribution to theosophical literature. Among his major works are *Human Nature, Look At Your Karma, The Eternal Truths of Life,* and *Man and His Seven Principles.*